Prepper Hacks Collection

3 Books to Help You Survive

I0417314

By Bill Shepherd

© 2015

Are You Prepared? For almost anything?

You know you need to be prepared. But maybe you don't know where to start? Maybe you consider yourself an expert prepper already. Maybe you're just a beginner. No matter how long you've been prepping, we all make mistakes. It's natural. It's human. But there are ways you can learn from others and avoid the same mistakes that we all make.

With this collection of 3 books, you'll learn how to be prepared for almost any event and how to survive for as long as you need to!

If you are interested in learning how to protect your family from any and all of the inevitable disasters that could potentially happen, this book is your first step to learning how to prepare for any emergency situation.

Don't wait - Get started today!

CONTENTS

Prepping for Disaster: Learn How to Survive Through the Worst Disasters

Introduction

We've all seen in on the news, from all over the world. An earthquake. A hurricane. An overthrow of the government. Armed citizens in the streets. Looting. Rioting. The list of bad things that can happen on any given day is almost endless. So what can you do?

Millions of Americans are now looking to prepare themselves for what the world has to throw at them. As crazy as it sounds, this isn't such a bad idea because, in today's world, you can never truly know what is waiting around the next corner.

It may be a scary thought for some but the world is a scary place and while most of us will remain relatively safe, many will not. Unfortunately there are disasters and they come with their own hidden dangers. However, being prepared for those dangers could potentially be the difference between living and dying.

Maybe you've already started prepping. Maybe you know you *need* to start, but you don't know *where* to start. If so, then this book is exactly what you need to begin your prepping journey and be truly ready to face anything that comes your way. Prepping doesn't have to mean living in an underground bunker full of bottled water, canned foods, and every weapon you can get your hands on. Prepping comes in all shapes and sizes and can be tailored for what you and your family really need. Prepping means different things to different people, and that's exactly the way you should approach it.

You may believe you're prepared for anything but are you *really* prepared? Let's get started.

Chapter One: Why Do You Need To Prepare For Emergencies And Natural Disasters?

Natural disasters and global emergencies aren't as rare as we think. Each year, there are thousands of disasters across the world and while most remain fairly minor, they still can be very deadly. Every disaster has its own pitfalls and those affected find themselves unprepared for the events. We see it on the news most nights, but we always think it couldn't happen to us. This is where we are wrong, and this is where prepping begins.

A weather storm may be predicted but you can't truly know the devastation it will cause; it's the same with a terror attack. An attack might be deadly but you can't predict or know how it will impact on your life or safety. Unfortunately, no one can predict what will happen even with the fancy security systems and weather forecast stations. Mother Nature is too unpredictable and, sometimes, everything comes down to human error. It might seem hopeless if you stop thinking there. But there *are* things you can do, steps you can take, to greatly increase your security and make sure that you and your family survive and thrive, no matter the situation.

In the end, being prepared for any eventuality allows you and those around you to take real steps to survive any horrors that might come your way as best as you possibly can.

Is Prepping Really Necessary?

This is a question that a lot of people ask, and a lot of preppers find themselves having to answer. Prepping is something very few people understand simply because they think it's a morbid or unnatural thought however, that is far from the truth. Preparing for disasters or government breakdown can be one of the smartest moves anyone can make today, simply because you're preparing for the worst.

This isn't about you *looking* for something awful to happen but rather, it's about preparing yourself and your family for anything, should a terrible tragedy occur. Disasters come in many forms, from tornadoes to terrorism and they occur at the least likely of times. Your home might appear safe but once disaster strikes, will it remain a safe haven?

No one wants to believe that anything bad will ever happen to them and their loved ones. Especially not when there is so much security out there. But, in a blink of an eye, the best security defenses can be torn down and left exposed. Thousands, if not millions, of people all around the world are not prepared for even the most minor of disasters, never mind the major ones. Sometimes, the minor disasters can cause the most problems and yet, most believe they're safe, when in reality, they are exposed to the worst elements possible.

Being unprepared is almost like ringing the dinner bell in a shark-feeding pen; you wouldn't want to be there when they come to feed. Being unprepared is simply asking for trouble. Prepping for disaster can appear to be an unnecessary and unhealthy obsession but no matter who you are or where you live, you must be fully prepared for any disaster that hits.

What Would Your First Thoughts Be When Tragedy Hits?

Take a moment to think about what your first thoughts or actions would be if and when a terrible disaster struck. Would you try to shore up the defenses in your home if you saw a local flood warning on TV or would you be scrambling for supplies and fighting through the crowds at the supermarket for the last bag of chips and bottled water? Would you leave your home when a terrorist attack happened in the State or would you seek shelter when a hurricane was heading your way?

The very first actions you take in a matter of seconds could determine your fate. No one thinks one hundred percent clearly at first when they hear about a minor flood or terror attack but being prepared allows you to get the shock out the way and get down to action. You will have things rehearsed and, though you will still be surprised or in shock, you will quickly revert to what you know, what you have trained for, and what you have taught yourself.

Your first instincts always will center on protecting the people and things that matter to you the most. However, sometimes, the warnings come too late and all you have is a few moments to decide your next move. When you're unprepared, you tend to make all of the wrong decisions because you spend most of the time packing up unnecessary belongings or calling around searching for help when you should just get out.

It is these simple precious seconds that could change the course of your life.

Everyone needs to be prepared so that if there is ever a time when they must survive without electricity or having drinking water, they know how to carry on and survive. Being prepared isn't something so-called crazy 'end-of-the-world' preachers are doing; everyday 9-5 people work to prepare fall-out shelters and are even ready to leave their home in a minute's notice.

Yes, it's very scary to think the worst can happen but the way you react will change everything and if you're unprepared, it's a nightmare.

Relying On Government Assistance Might Not Be a Possibility
Government responses during emergencies can be phenomenally good, but, as we saw with Hurricane Katrina, it comes much too late in some instances. This isn't designed to scare you because while the government has an excellent response time, it doesn't guarantee you food shelter or safety. Simply put: you can't rely on the government to take care of you in a disaster situation.

Major disasters cause a great deal of problems for the government, both on a local level and on a federal level. Roads can become inaccessible and resources might be very tight. The unfortunate truth is that while the government pulls out every stop possible to help those affected by whatever tragedy strikes, there can be time delays and lack of communication, resulting in problems for us average citizens.

Any rescue worker will understand how difficult it is to reach everyone in danger and you must understand that too, because you cannot solely rely on the government to help you. They may be able to provide additional shelter for you as well as food and water but when will that be? It could be days or possibly even weeks before you receive help and that could be too late. Do you really want to leave your survival in the hands of someone else?

The fault doesn't lie with the government or with the local police, fire and ambulance service; it's just an unfortunate trap that accompanies tragedy. You have to remember, thousands may be waiting for help but there may not be enough resources for everyone. This is why you *must* be prepared to take care of yourself and your loved ones. If you don't, who will?

However, crisis' can bring out the best in people too because those able can lend a hand to help dig out people buried in rubble and race to people struggling to stay afloat in flooded waters. Food parcels can be organized and local shelters are set up; and while this is a wonderful show of strength and community, they don't always arrive quickly.

Every situation is different, whether you're left facing a bush-fire in the Californian desert or a tornado whisking its way to Detroit. However, most think they should just prepare for natural disasters or terrorism and nothing else. But, clearly, this isn't the case, because rioting, civil violence and even simple power cuts can cause major incidents too. You have to be as prepared for civil violence as prepared for a terrorist attack or a natural disaster, because they can all be just as deadly and as frightening.

Getting support, food and shelter to every person affected can be a challenge, especially in remote areas. Sometimes, the minor incidents don't get contributions from the State as bigger incidents do. Governments can help but they aren't always able to and that is one of the biggest reasons why you must think about ways to help protect yourself and those around you.

Chapter Two: The Essentials to Prepare For a Natural Disaster and Stay Safe

Natural disasters are as unpleasant as they are unpredictable. Sometimes, what looks like an average storm suddenly turns into a wild and deadly disaster and it's these events you have to be prepared for. Will you know what to do when Mother Nature strikes? Of course you will, because you're a prepper! And if you're prepared, you'll be far ahead of the 95% of the population who will have no idea what to do.

Finding Shelter and Water Supplies

The body is a complicated thing because while it can go potentially weeks without food, it simply must have water to survive. You may be able to go a day or two without water but then, slowly and surely, the body starts to feel the impact. Dehydration begins to kick in and then the full force of water starvation is felt. Dehydration poses a significant risk to life and when you drink dirty water, it can cause severe health problems too. So how to prepare?

During natural disasters, it's especially difficult to find a supply of safe drinking water. However, you can avoid the struggle for water by stocking up your home. You can easily buy three or four gallons of bottled water from a local store and keep it safely in a storage cupboard until it's needed.

If you live in an area which floods annually, then it's especially a good idea to have your own supply of drinking water. It will come in quite handy, should the local supply be cut off or be unsafe to consume.

However, for shelter, you need to choose a suitable location to stay during the crisis. Ideally you want to remain indoors and your home is the best bet. Sometimes, it won't be safe to stay in if there is severe flooding or hurricanes approaching. For minor disasters such as power cuts and light hail storms, the home is probably the safest option possible.

If you choose the home as your shelter you need to inspect the property and see what shape it's in. There may be a few upgrades needed to help keep the home safe during violence storms and if that is the case, don't be afraid to spend the money to protect the home. Hopefully you'll never need shelter but if you do, then the home is there and ready.

However, if the home isn't a safe option or you wish to have a secondary shelter in place, you could choose a local community center, a friend's home, a family member residence or even a bunker. There are lots of good options open to you so don't be afraid to explore all possibilities and find the safest shelter available to you.

Setting up a P.O.A

A P.O.A. or plan of action has become one of the best if not, basic survival tools to have to survive a natural disaster. These plans are great because you cover escape routes, shelters and the steps you'd take to protect yourself when a storm is brewing. However, this can be used for any disaster and creating a plan can be very easy to do.

The first step to prepare your Plan of Action would be to assess your home. There could potentially be several high-risk factors lurking around your home and these factors need to be addressed and dealt with quickly. So, let's say you lived in an area where bush-fires broke out occasionally; you would want to assess your property and the surrounding area.

Do you have any overgrown shrubbery or trees that might catch fire? Is there excessive rubbish on the property that could cause a fire to spread? It's these types of things that need to be assessed and addressed quickly when it comes to preparing and possibly even avoiding disaster.

Protecting Property

As much as you want to protect the items inside your home, you also need to think about outside. If there is any garden furniture outside, you have to either bring it in or secure it down so that it cannot cause any damage. Garbage cans and heavy potted plants may need to be placed indoors to prevent them from flying into cars and properties. Anything outside that isn't nailed down should be brought inside and secured in a room; of course, some items aren't suitable for indoors but those items would need to be secured as best as you possibly can outdoors.

For vehicles and automobiles, it would be much wiser to lock them up safely in the garage to keep any damage to a minimal. If you do not have a garage, you need to find a safe location for the vehicle so that it doesn't get damaged; you could always park the car in an elevated spot if flooding is predicted.

Windows and doors also need to stay locked and bolted. All shutters need to be closed and the blinds and drapes must be closed too. For heavy winds or storms, you could even look to boarding the windows and doors up with heavy wooden boards to help prevent them from breaking and shattering. Doors can be braced up with heavier objects during heavy storms; however, you could look at impact resistant window glass. Impact resistant windows are a lot more expensive but they can be quite effective at the same time.

If there is flooding expected, it would be much better to start moving items from the lower floors of the home into the second floor. Valuables can be stored in rooms higher up and expensive furniture can be moved upstairs or somewhere the water cannot get to it. This should also include your insurance documents – these should be stored in a water and fireproof locked box in a dry location.

Create Your Emergency Kit

You cannot prepare for a disaster without creating an emergency kit. This is an essential part of surviving because should you ever have to leave your home, you have the emergency kit all ready and waiting. There are companies who pre-make emergency kits but it's much better to build one yourself.

This isn't stocking up a huge pile of food or water but rather the necessary items you'll need during an emergency. When preparing your kit, have a three-day supply of fresh and preferably warm clothing as well as several maps of the local area. There should also be a flashlight with extra batteries, a battery-powered radio, a first aid kit, blankets, sanitation items; and there should be food and water rations for at least three days. A whistle can also be useful to attract help.

To be honest, an emergency kit can grow and grow but you should just have the bare essentials so it can be picked up and moved quickly. You might need to go on the move and you can't have an emergency kit that weighs hundreds of pounds otherwise, you won't get far.

It can also be a good idea to have an emergency kit stored in your car just in case a disaster strikes when you're out of the home. The car kit can basically hold the same items with the exception of maybe spare cash to help find a safe way home.

Have a First Aid Kit for Injuries

A first aid kit can be so useful to have at hand when someone is hurt and help can't get through. Of course, a first aid kit isn't going to offer the same type of equipment a doctor has but it will offer some of the essential items. You can have a good stock of medical bandages, sterile dressings, antibiotic hand wash, a thermometer, simple aspirin and pain relief medicines and scissors medical tape.

All of these items can be very important to have during a natural disaster for minor cuts and injuries. The kit might just allow you to help someone until medical help is able to get to you.

Always Carry Extra Fuel for the Car

You can't predict what you'll need to do during a crisis and it might be that leaving your home is a must. However, your vehicle absolutely must be fully gassed up at all times. You can't stop off at gas stations to fill up because they will be a nightmare and it's quite possible, there will be no gas or fuel available in miles.

Instead, you can store anything up to twenty gallons for an emergency. However, the gas shouldn't be stored anywhere inside the home for safety. Keep the extra fuel in a safe location where only you know of it.

Communication Is a Must

Most people own a cell phone today and you must have at least one fully charged up phone with you at all times no matter where you go. It might be a good idea to buy a second cheap but reliable cell phone and store it in the car or in an emergency kit should you ever need it. Also, keep a second charger in the emergency kit.

Landlines can be just as good as cell phones, if not a little more reliable however, they might not be working still which is why a cell phone is a must. However, phones aren't the only options to consider to keep in contact with the outside world you can also use computers.

Prepare the Home

You will need a supply of food for the upcoming days, if not weeks, which means you have to do a lot of stocking up. Now, water can be bought over time and stored until it's needed but for foods, it's a little different because some can go out-of-date quickly. So, it's best to stick with canned goods as well as simple everyday foods such as crackers and cereals and even chocolate bars.

Should the power go out and you're stuck in home, you have a few options for food. For the refrigerator items, you can eat them first as long as you eat them within the first few hours of the power going off. For any food item that looks questionable, don't eat it. After three or four hours, the food in the refrigerator might not be good enough to eat so dispose of them and move onto your canned goods and long lasting snacks.

Frozen foods can still be consumed but it's not always advisable. If you plan to eat meat that's thawing from the freezer, it should be cooked thoroughly and consumed immediately. However, if the power has been off for a considerable amount of time, you should not consume any foods whatsoever for safety reasons. Sometimes, it's best to stick to your food rations.

Another important factor to remember is checking on your fire blankets and extinguishers regularly. Now, these items should be stored at various points in the home and they need to be checked on ever few months. If you can, have a fire extinguisher or fire blanket on every floor in the home and possibly every room especially in high-risk areas such as the kitchen.

When the electricity goes out, you are going to have very limited options. You cannot use any electric item, which means it's difficult to get a read on the events outside because if the modem is down you can't get online. You can still use battery-powered radios, which will give you some necessary updates so remember to have your radios at the ready.

Have Cash at the Ready

Stashing a huge sum of cash in the home isn't always a good idea but it's a wise move to have a little cash ready. Emergencies can often lead to a rush to the local ATM machines and in a panic, banks can be closed for several reasons, which could potentially leave you with little or no cash. However, if you have a small amount of cash in your home, you have at least something to use.

Get To Higher Ground and Stay Safe

For areas that receive severe flooding, it would be best to look for higher ground. If you are staying within your home, you should retreat to the upper floors. It might not be wise to head into the attic unless you feel totally safe about that area of the home. However, if you aren't staying within the home due to rising floodwaters, you need to find safety with higher ground. You can head to local shelters or areas which are safe from flood waters but remember to stay safe when evacuating your home.

When the storm hits outside, you should find the safest room within your shelter. Ideally, the room would have little or no windows and it would have enough space to hold the family comfortably until the crisis is over. There should be at least one room in the home or shelter that is suitable to ride the storm out.

Do not use any form of electricity when it comes to a natural disaster. If there is flooding, no matter how minor it could cause serious injury to you and may lead to fire. Also, if you're leaving the home, follow all safety instructions and find the safest and quickest route out.

Get Insurance

Everyone has their own thoughts about insurance and while most will have some sort of insurance on the property or valuables, you might not. It's really your choice whether or not you want to insure your property; it could be a good idea but it's down to you. If your home is regularly flooded then insurance prices might be higher but you'll have to do some checking.

Chapter Three: How to Survive Civil Violence and Power Outages

Pandemonium can break out at the least expected of times and while your hometown might appear safe, the situation can change quickly. Civil unrest and violence occurs more than you think and it can have huge repercussions for all involved even if you aren't directly involved with any violence. A simple power shortage might even cause civil unrest to break out and you must know how to survive.

Stock Up On Supplies When You Hear Of Problems

If you have an emergency kit already stored in your home, that can be very useful but civil unrest and violence can carry on for weeks at a time. You will need more supplies so, whenever you hear of unrest at the next town over, it's time to get stocked up. It's the same if you hear about upcoming marches or protests in your local area; your first port of call should be to the local grocery store and then the hardware store.

It doesn't hurt to spend a little extra cash on supplies such as canned goods, energy bars, protein bars, crackers, jams, jellies, canned fruits and simple snacks that are long lasting. There are plenty of good foods out there that last a considerable time so look for things you and your family will eat – and don't forget extra bottled water!

However, don't make it obvious you're stocking up on supplies because word will get out and there'll be a panic. Instead, casually shop and if that means going to a few stores, so be it; just make sure you have enough food and water supplies to last for the upcoming days. Remember, civil violence and even a power cut can last week's so be prepared for longer problems.

Plan Your Home Route

When a power shortage strikes or violence breaks out, it would be much easier to lock the doors and stay inside until the chaos passes but what happens if you or your family are out? Well, it can be a very frightening time but if you ever find yourself away from the home during civil violence, you have to plan your next move.

Ideally you want to get back home to where it's safe or to where your family is, so you want to set out your plan to get home. You know the local area and you probably already know what routes you'll take when you're at work or the shops but the direct routes mightn't be possible to take. You will need to have several back-up routes home so that when disaster strikes, you can safely find your way home.

Everyone in your family should have their own routes devised so that they are able to make their way home safely and without being caught up in the violence. Of course, you would prefer to be locked safely indoors when a power cut happens or when civil unrest breaks-out but it isn't always going to be that way. However, when you devise your safety routes home, you will hopefully avoid danger as best as you can.

Don't be afraid to learn the home routes by heart and if you have to, go on dry runs so you can get the routes planted in your mind for whenever you need them. Every member of your family should do this and don't forget to add a route to school to pick up the children. Younger children shouldn't be heading out alone during civil unrest and even some older children shouldn't be venturing out alone either.

Ditch the Car When You're Faced with Roaming Dangers and Blocked Roads

Experts say it's best to stay where you are during civil unrest because it's too dangerous to go outdoors. However, it isn't a wise idea to sit in your car in the middle of civil unrest either, especially when there are mobs romancing the streets. Mobs can be very dangerous and while they aren't there to intentionally cause you harm, you might inadvertently get in the way.

Things can spiral out of control very quickly and you don't want to be there when a mob turns on you or your vehicle. You don't want to leave your car behind but if the road becomes blocked, congested or impassible, then it's time to ditch the car and head on home on foot.

If you can, store a backpack with an emergency cell phone, some cash, water and a map of the local area. They will help get your home and remember to lock up the car; it might not do a great deal to protect it but if you can, park it in a safe area if possible.

Seek Shelter from Safety

Power cuts and civil unrest can be very much the same – looters come out to play as well as a lot of unsavory characters – and being caught amongst them can be scary. If you find yourself away from the safety of your home, you need to try and find shelter; somewhere that is safe and secure from trouble brewing outside.

You could seek shelter at a family or colleague's home or even at a local community center; police stations might be a bit chaotic but most police officers are willing to help innocent people trying to seek shelter from the violence outside. Even in a power cut, police officers would be willing to offer a helping hand to those stuck with no means of getting home.

If you find yourself far away from the home and no other shelters are available, you still need to keep a low profile. Try to stay away from crowded areas and take a safe route home; if you are really stuck in the middle of nowhere, seek shelter where you can, even if that means ducking in and out of alleyways and abandoned buildings. Ideally you'd have a shelter in place but if not, don't panic and seek shelter where you can.

Stay Indoors At All Costs

Going outside when there is a riot or power cut outside can be very, very dangerous for you. You could put yourself in harm's way by getting caught up in rioting, violence and even looting; you certainly do not want to be there when that happens. It's best for you and your family's safety to stay inside.

The best move for you is to hunker down in your shelter. You should lock and secure all doors and windows and board up any potential entry also. For those living in a condo or an apartment should maybe consider adding double locks to the doors and windows and even maybe blocking the entry points with heavy objects so that should someone try to gain entry, they won't be able to. Barricading yourself in might be extreme but if things get out of control, it's a possibility – just remember to remain indoors at all times.

Stock Up On Medicines and Medical Supplies

You don't know how long you're going to be stuck indoors when civil violence breaks-out and you have to be prepared for every possible problem. It would be a good idea to have all of the family's prescriptions filled and up-to-date and stored so that you don't run out of much needed and potentially life-saving medication or medicines.

Also, you have to think about having an extra supply of medical bandages, disposable gloves, hand gels, plasters and all other necessary medical supplies. Your emergency kit should have your first aid kits but if you choose not to opt for the emergency kit, try to set up your own home first aid kit to deal with injuries. The most important point to remember is stocking up on prescriptions such as allergy medicines, diabetes medication and other life-threatening medications.

Avoid Crowded Areas and the Hot Zone

The number one rule to deal with civil violence is to avoid overly crowded areas! The hot zone is going to be at the epicenter of the chaos and you do not want to find yourself in these areas whatsoever. The hot zone presents the worst of the worst trouble and being caught here can be very dangerous for you to deal with.

Instead, do your best to avoid the hot zone and crowded areas as much as possible. However, if you do find yourself in crowded areas that are full of trouble, you need to keep a level head. Don't get caught up in the chaos; try to slip away from these areas and get indoors and stay there until the trouble is over.

Don't Resist Arrest if you're caught Up With Protesters

Hopefully you'll be indoors but if you somehow manage to find yourself outside and in the middle of a riot, you have to be smart. Police are going to be swarming everywhere and if you find yourself being taken into custody, don't struggle and don't resist! The charges might just be breach of the peace but if you struggle or try to resist you might get additional charges that are much worse.

As said, you really should be indoors but if you get caught up while on the way home, follow the officers instructions at all times. The best advice for being outdoors – don't be there!

Be Wary Of Roadblocks

When there is severe civil violence outside, there can be checkpoints and roadblocks set up along the major highways and roads to help stamp out looters and protesters. However, some checkpoints might not have been set up by police, but rather, by those looking for trouble. If you can, avoid the roadblocks as much as possible.

Have a Back-Up Plan in Place

If your home is a no-go area or right in the epicenter, you might be best to seek alternative shelter. It might simply not be safe to head back home for the foreseeable future and if that's the case, you have to find another shelter, which is safe for you to remain in which the disruptions outside continue.

It might be possible to seek shelter with a neighbor, a family member or even a friend. There should always be a back-up plan in place when you need shelter and even if it's taking cover at the local library, so be it, as long as it's safe.

Avoid Everyone and Trust Your Instincts

During unrest there can be a lot of mobs, gangs and groups around looking to cause trouble and you want to avoid them all. In fact, during crisis times, you really want to avoid as much people as possible, if not them all because any one person can be dangerous. It's crazy to say but a person can react completely different during a riot than what they would during a normal day and its best to avoid everyone.

Also, your instincts might tell you to do one thing and you should follow those instincts because they might just help to keep you safe. If your instincts are telling you to remain indoors, do it; or if they're telling you to avoid making a lot of noise, don't make any noise!

Putting Up Defenses for Your Home As Long As You Can

How you choose to defend your home depends entirely on your thoughts and feelings. While you might have a right to bear arms and protect your family, it's your choice whether that is right for you. To be honest, some people will say they don't want firearms in their home and that is up to them and their right; and vice versa for those who want to carry arms. However, if you should choose to defend your home using a weapon, please be very careful with it and most importantly understand how to use it.

If you choose not to carry a weapon, you can still defend the home. For a start, you should secure every possible entry point from the garage door to the basement window. There are dozens of potential entry points and you must secure them all; it might sound a little stupid but your doggy doors needs to be fairly secured as well. You can easily board up the windows from the outside as well as on the inside too, close the shutters on the outside and barricade the doors.

However, if you are not able to defend the home for whatever reason, have your escape route planned. Don't put yourself in harm's way to save your home because it could cost you your life so use the best judgment and if you feel it's time to leave, find a safe exit and head towards another shelter if you can.

Staying Safe Inside during a Power Cut or Riot

It's very easy to say that since you live in a remote area, its unlikely major rioting will flare up and while that is possible, it's not a guarantee. What is more, even if there isn't violence where you reside that doesn't mean the impact from the rioting in major cities won't eventually cause disruption for you. Remote areas can at times be hit hard even when it isn't affected directly by violence; you cannot be complacent into believing there won't be any disruption to food or water supplies.

Also, if you plan to travel anywhere in the local or wider communities, you need to research how safe the areas are. Keep a close eye on proceedings locally and on a broad aspect too so that you can be totally sure how safe the towns and cities are. It would help to keep an eye over weather conditions too.

Whether you plan to travel or just want to prepare for impending disaster, it's important to keep an eye out for signs. Now, some signs might be very obvious and on television there are threats of violence made and if you spot trouble brewing, get your supplies at the ready.

Chapter Four: Creating the Perfect Bug-Out Bag

Leaving your home in a second's notice can be very tense. However, a bug-out bag can become the number one tool to rely on during a disaster. Though, hundreds of people aren't really sure what they need to equip with their bug-out bag. So, what should you kit your bug-out bag with?

How to Create Your Bug-Out Bag

Ideally your bug-out bag should contain enough supplies and materials to last you for the upcoming days. You might need to leave the home for days at a time and it needs to be well stocked and prepared for any occasion.

The bug-out bag may be a little heavier than an emergency kit but you are using more than just the basic supplies. The bag should have enough items for surviving between eight and ten days outside the home. Now, you can go all out and get very serious here and stock up with tons and tons of emergency supplies but, let's face it, it's difficult to take it all with you anywhere. The bug-out bag is designed to be easy to carry but effectively kitted out so don't go crazy and overstuff the bag with unnecessary items.

The best place to start your bug-out bag is with the food and water supply. You need at least one liter of water each day, so you should have four or five liters of bottled water in your bag. If you plan to get water from other sources outside the home, you'll need to use a water filter system to help make it safe to drink. Now, you could choose the old-fashioned means of boiling the water with iodine tablets which would sanitize the water and make it suitable to consume. For this method, you'll need to have a pack of iodine tablets and a small saucepan – and don't forget the safety matches!

For foods, canned goods such as canned meat, tuna, canned fruits and peanut butter make great items to opt for. However, you can also choose quinoa, barley, kidney beans, lentils, pasta and cornmeal too; and powdered milk and candy can also be suitable options. Of course, canned goods can be heavy so you might want to look at packet foods and only pack three or four canned items. You can add more if you are able to carry more but don't overload the bag with canned foods; and remember to take along light cooking equipment such as a skillet or saucepan.

The bag must also be equipped with a tent or warm blankets; and you should also have a thick tarp to shield you from rain, sleet and snow. There may come a time when you have to sleep outdoors or spend a period outside and you must have some form of shelter to help protect you from the elements. Even if you have a tent, you can still take a tarp with you and prop it up and it can act as a shelter.

Next, you must have two or three changes of suitable, warm clothing with you. Ideally you would have two or three warm jumpers, a few pairs of thick or durable pants and a few pairs of t-shirts or undershirts and clean underwear. However, you cannot forget about suitable footwear. You should have thick, heavy boots suitable for any and all road conditions. Men and women can both use walking boots and remember to ditch less durable footwear like sneakers and high heels.

All bug-out bags need to have some sort of first aid kits. Now, you can easily pick up a kit from a local pharmacy or make one from scratch. If you don't want to spend the time putting together your own first aid kit then buy a basic kit and add it into your bag.

Don't forget to pack additional maps of the local area!

Prepare and Keep Your Bag Close

Now you know how to prepare your bug-out bag, it's time to let you in on a few secrets. One of the biggest errors most people make is to know how to prepare their bags but don't get around assembling it. Now, while you might think you'll have time to sort everything out later on, you might find that's a terrible idea. You can't know what is coming around the corner and it might be that you don't have three minutes so your bag must be ready and all prepared.

You can't be rushing around throwing your bug-out bag together; it should be packed and stored safely, somewhere you can easily get to it. If you can, create a second bug-out bag and store it in the car of the office should you be unable to get home for it. Occasionally update the bag to check on the food and throw in new clothes if you outgrow your clothes.

Remember, the whole point of the bug-out bag is to leave with it in seconds so don't go putting it somewhere you can't get to it.

Create A Meeting Place during an Emergency

Bugging out in a matter of seconds can be made a lot simpler once you have a plan of escape set up. Now, you probably know all the escape routes in your home but what about after you leave, where will you go? Well, this is something you have to prepare for because if you have no central meeting point then you'll be going around in circles.

Remember, internet and phone lines may be down and if you're separated from your family members, then at least you all know where your meeting place is. Your location can be something as simple as your front lawn or even a town hall; but no matter where your meeting point is, ensure everyone knows how to get to it. There is no point in creating an escape plan without having a meeting place in mind.

Minor emergencies need escape plans and a safe meeting location just as the major emergencies. However, when you're creating your escape plan and meeting place, try to ensure it's going to be safe for everyone to get to. It might be a good idea to have a central meeting point where every family member knows about as well as a second meeting place that can be used as a fallback position.

Don't Delay In Leaving

Your bugging out for a reason – it's dangerous to stay where you are – so don't delay in moving out. Yes, it's hard to leave everything you own behind but for safety, you have to. You never know, when you return, the home might still be in the same position as you left it but you can't delay leaving when there is a major disaster.

If you hear the three-minute warning or if a hurricane is heading your way, get out! Take your bug-out bag, get into your car and leave as fast as you can.

Set Up Several Evacuation Routes for Leaving Your Home

There are usually a few major roads leading in and out of a town and while your first thought is to take these routes – think again. When a major incident occurs and everyone is heading out of town, all of the major routes out will be backlogged and chock full of vehicles and people looking to escape the disaster. These routes aren't going to be accessible at the best of times and you need to search for alternative routes.

It's vital to have several escape routes planned and set out. You could look at the minor or smaller routes to take you out of the city, which might take you a little longer to leave, but they could be worth their weight in gold. You should have one alternative route set out and if that one fails to work out, have another and another. Ideally, you should have several evacuation routes set up so that if one or two fails, there is always another back-up road out.

Of course, if you know your way around the local area then you probably already know what routes to take. If you don't know the local area, its best to keep a map with you at all times and consult it should an emergency arise when you're out and about or travelling to an unknown area.

Chapter Five: Surviving Any Disaster – What Steps To Take To Keep the Family Safe

Your family is the people you care about most of all. You would do anything for them and you'd ensure their safety no matter what but how would you keep them safe during a crisis? You might have a plan for the local weather but what happens when a Nation-wide disaster strikes, would you still be able to keep your family safe?

Don't panic, because there are hundreds of other families in the same boat as you and while it may be a scary task to keep your family protected, it doesn't need to be impossible. Here are some simple but effective ways to help prepare your family for the worst events imaginable and help keep them safe.

Be Prepared For a Terror Attack

There is no simple or mathematical theory to predict an act of terrorism, unfortunately. This is one of the worst atrocities and yet, you can be prepared should it ever happen near you. It might not be easy but you can always be prepared for whatever comes your way.

If your local town, city or district suddenly finds itself the center of a terror attack, the best thing for you to do is lock your doors and stay inside. Now, if you live on the edge of town, it's unlikely you'll be affected as much as those who live in the epicenter. However, if you live a fair distance away from the attack, you should remain indoors and secure the building whether it's in the form of a chemical attack or any other attack.

For those who live within the epicenter of the attack, you have a few options; the first being evacuating the home. Now, evacuation might not be necessary unless your home is at risk from the effects of the attack or that it's simply not safe for you to remain there. If that is the case, grab your bug-out bag or emergency kit and leave and get to safety. You can take shelter at a local hospital if you require treatment or stay with a family member if you aren't hurt.

The second option for you would be to remain indoors. Now, this might be a solution if it's unsafe to leave the home. If you cannot leave then hunker down in the home and secure all doors and windows until help arrives. This might not be the best solution but if its unsafe to go outside, you must remain protected at all times.

If an attack occurs while you're out of the home or out of the city, you will need to get out of the danger zone. This can be often difficult don't try not to panic. It's easier said than done I know however, in these awful times, its best to keep your head so that you can get out of the danger zone and head to safety.

For those who plan to get out of the city or the danger zone, you have to be wary of the local area. Buildings might be unstable so, watch for falling debris and be wary of any unsavory characters. If you wish to stay and help those who have been hurt, that's great on you but you still need to remain vigilant.

Head to Your Fall-Out Shelter after Biological or Chemical Incidents

Fall-out shelters have become such a driving force of late and more and more people are now choosing to buy one especially for their family. You could always make a little purchase of a fall-out shelter and during biological or chemical incidents, retreat to here.

It's a good place to ride out the storm and hopefully you'll remain safe there. However, if you are going to use a fall-out shelter, take some supplies for the upcoming weeks and have battery powered radios to keep up-to-date with the latest news.

Evacuate the Town If Necessary

It isn't just necessary to evacuate when a terrorist attack strikes but also some natural disasters. For a start, violent thunderstorms and severe flooding might call for you to evacuate the local area. If this is something the government or local authority advises, do so quickly but calmly.

Follow the State's advice and don't delay in getting out. If you don't have any transport to leave, the government might be able to organize public transport and if you are considered a vulnerable person, there should be some organized help for you to evacuate.

However, if you can, band up with a neighbor or family member and pull resources together.

Work With Vulnerable People And Give Them A Leg Up!

There are lots of vulnerable people out there from elderly residents to handicap individuals and when there is a disaster; they may find it considerably harder to stay safe. Now, the local authorities can't help everyone however, if you see anyone in need of help or know-of someone who may need additional help, why not offer your services? There is no harm in going around to a neighbor and check on their safety and well being.

This isn't about earning brownie points or gold stars but rather ensuring the safety of others around you.

Secure Up the Home

Inspect the home in regular periods. Check on every inch of the home from the foundations to the roof and everything in-between. You want to ensure the home has no faults and if there is anything which might need to be repaired to help secure the home, do it.

There are plenty of ways to help secure the home too including having impact resistant glass on the windows and extra locks on the door. A dead-bolt can be good to help when there is rioting outside as well as storm storms and winds and keeping outdoor furniture indoors during storms or securing them down.

Use Coolers to Store Foods during Blackouts

When the power goes out, you have a few options to keep your perishable yogurts, cheeses and dairy products fresh. The best and only real option would be to use a cooler but again, these would only work for a few hours after the fridge goes out. However, if you can, eat as much food that is going to get spoiled within the first few hours so that it doesn't all go to waste.

If the power is going to be off for a while, you can start off with the fridge items and then move onto your supplies within your home. You should still have your emergency rations and preserves stored away so before you start on these, you can finish off whatever you have lying around that's still edible. However, don't eat anything from the refrigerator after three or four hours.

To help keep open packet foods fresh, store them in sealable containers.

Filter All Drinking Water

For water coming straight out of a sealed bottle, you shouldn't have many problems with it; however, if you choose to get drinking water from a tap, you need to take steps to make it safe. Now, you can go the older method of boiling the water before using it or you can also buy a water filtration system, which can be very useful. These systems can be a bit costly but they can be worth it if you can get your hands on one of these.

Use Any Alternative Power Source Available

Backup generators have to be one of the best alternative power sources to rely on. Now, if you're lucky enough to have one, use it because it might just help to get you through the upcoming days. Backup generators can be a bit costly at the best of times but during extended blackouts or power cuts, they can be so useful.

However, you can also rely on solar energy. This isn't going to be for everyone but if you already have solar energy panels in your home then it could help to power the home until normal electrical supplies are restored.

Chapter Six: Simple Steps to Keep the Family Safe during an Earthquake

Earthquakes are one of the most frequent disasters most towns and cities face in America today and they can be just as deadly as any other disaster out there. An earthquake might appear fairly minor but you can't predict how much damage it will cause. There have been earthquakes that cause power lines to come down as well as cause holes in roads to appear – the potential damage is unknown but very deadly.

Here are a few steps to help protect your family during and after an earthquake.

Identify Hazards within Your Home and Property

First and foremost, you have to know what the potential hazards and dangers there are. The exterior needs to be assessed; if there is garden furniture, look to see whether it's close to the property as well as whether it's likely to do damage.

Next, head into your garage and look at where your car is parked. Are there any hanging shelves in the garage that could break and cause damage to the car? Well, if there is, you need to think about securing the shelves better or move the car to an area of the garage that doesn't have any hanging objects.

For the interior of the home, you have lots of issues on hand. Now, for ornaments and little trinkets on tables, windowsills and shelves, you can't really do much with these because you can't predict an earthquake. However, you can secure moveable objects instead such as water or boil tanks, unstable shelves and bookcases. It's strange but there are several dangerous items in your home that need to be secured better should an earthquake hit.

Take a good look around the home, inside and out; and identify what hazards there are as well as the steps to take to make the home more secure. Things will get damaged and broken but they can be easily replaced; heavier items need to be secured down as best as possible.

Decide Your Safe Areas in the Home and Have a Plan Ready
Mostly, when an earthquake occurs, you head into the doorways to protect yourself but you should still have designated safe areas in the home. This can be a room that doesn't have items or objects hanging on the wall. However, you should also set up an emergency plan for an earthquake just in case you find yourself unable to get to a safe location.

Place Your Rations in Convenient Spots
You probably have all of your supplies and rations at the ready but how easy are they to get to? It's important to keep all of your rations and supplies in convenient areas where you and your family can easily get to without venturing far. Now, if you have a one-floor

home, look at placing the rations in the master bedroom so that it's the central location.

For an up and downstairs home, you might want to store them in a central area such as a cupboard in the den or front living room. However, the supplies should be accessible for all.

Take Cover

When an earthquake hits, you must find cover. You could stay in a doorway to avoid falling objects or if you can't get to a doorway, take cover under a strong table. Don't stand underneath shelves because you could be hurt from falling objects.

Clean Up and Record the Incident

After the earthquake has struck, you have the duty of cleaning up whatever damage has been caused. If there is considerable damage inside, clean up and if there is damage to the property, clean up the glass, board the windows and take pictures for insurance claims.

Chapter Seven: Survivalist Tips You Can Use In Real Life Situations

Emergencies and crisis' are never pleasant but they will come at some point. Being prepared may just allow you to avoid serious injury, if not keep your family safe. However, most people don't like to think about disasters or emergencies affecting them.

That is a stupid way to think because something will come your way at least once in your lifetime, whether it's a minor flood, an extended power cut or even (hopefully never) a terror attack. If you aren't prepared for these events, it could cost you your life so being prepared; even just a little prepared could save you or your family's life. Of course, you shouldn't go around being afraid of what will happen but at the same time, you shouldn't be totally unprepared either.

You need to have a balance between being prepared and being worried because while a disaster might come around once in your life, it's still vital to prepare for it. You could end up putting your life at serious risk just because you didn't prepare for such events.

Don't Panic, Keep a Calm Head

It's very easy for someone to sit and say when a disaster strikes, you should remain calm but going out of your mind with fear is never good idea. You must remain as calm as possible and keep a level head, if only to help get you and your family to a safe zone.

Crazy things happen and while you might be in a safe town now, that could change in a blink of an eye. If you're unprepared for any emergency or disaster then you'll end up panicking and doing all the wrong things. Instead, take a moment to take a deep breath, assess the situation and get your thinking cap on!

Add To Your Food Rations Whenever You Can
Your home can have a nice little food supply cupboard all ready and prepared for when things take a turn for the worst and you shouldn't be afraid to continue to add to it. Now, you might think you have enough food but you don't know how long you might need to be indoors for and it doesn't hurt to have enough.

Of course, if some foods are about to expire then use them in your daily meals and replace them. Canned goods usually last a very long time so you probably don't have to worry too much about these. However, for backpack meals and packets of foods, you might need to take a closer look at them every so often.

Though, whenever you are out at the grocery store, why not pick up an extra item or two and add that into your ration cupboard. You should do the same with water as well as batteries and medical supplies. If you continue to do this, whenever there is an emergency you have enough supplies to see you through until help arrives or until it's safe to go outdoors.

Have a Contingency Plan

You might have your escape and evacuation plans all set out and prepared but what happens if a spanner is thrown into the works? Well, you might need to alter the plan somewhere and if you aren't prepared for this then it can go downhill fast.

Instead, you should set out several plans so that if one should fail or be unusable, there is another to work with.

Work With Others

It doesn't matter if you're a single person or have a family unit; you still need to consider working with the people around you. Remember, there are going to be others out there who don't have anyone to rely on and have no supplies at hand and while you may not have a huge amount yourself, it can be good to help someone in need. You shouldn't give away all you've worked for but you can share and you never know you might be able to pull in precious resources you don't have.

A group unit can have a better chance of survival than one man on his own simply because there are more resources available. You should always consider working with others whom you trust and you can rely on also.

Disasters Happens – Don't Shy Away

Let's face it, disasters will happen whether they are major or minor and help might not come. It's your chance to sit up, take charge and survive whatever is out there. This is never going to be easy and it won't be pleasant but if you shy away or rely on others to help you, you might be in for a nasty surprise.

You have to be the person who stands up and really takes the reins so that you survive and make it to safety. It's easy to let someone else handle the work but that mightn't always be an option for you. Instead of shying away, get ready, be prepared and handle whatever disaster comes your way.

Conclusion

Thank you to all who took the time to read this book. I hope you have enjoyed reading and know a little more about prepping for disaster.

This wasn't meant to scare anyone but rather help those wants to learn more about prepping for impending disasters as well as hopefully help anyone survive should they find themselves in a dangerous situation.

Good luck, fellow preppers!

*****

A Prepper's Stockpile: *A Simple Guide to Help You Prepare For Disaster*

Introduction

Stockpiling for a disaster might seem a little morbid to some, however, it can become one of the best tools you rely on to survive during trying times. This isn't just about being prepared for the little disasters when you're left without power for an hour or two, but is more geared towards actual, real long-term emergencies and disasters that can change your life. Wars, natural disasters, terrorism, political and social instability – there are a hundred different scenarios where you might need to be prepared to survive on your own. Starting a Prepper's Pantry is one of the first steps you can take towards becoming self-sufficient and providing for you and your family, no matter what.

It can often seem frightening and scary to think about preparing for some sort of nation-wide emergency but it is really an important task to do. In today's world, there are disasters around every corner and you really never know what is going to affect your daily life. One minute you could be sitting in a well-built house with your family and the next, a tornado rips it all away. It could happen, and it has. We see it on the news every day. But most of us think "it'll never happen to us". Preppers, on the other hand, think, "It *could* happen. But I *will* be prepared!"

That is why everyone should learn how to stockpile emergency supplies and be prepared for whatever dangers appear. This book will teach you the basics to building a Prepper's Stockpile: which items to store, how to store them, and tips and tricks for building up the best possible survival pantry that you can. At the end of the book, you'll have a good start towards safety, self-sufficiency, protection, and freedom for you and your loved ones.

So, let's get started!

Chapter One: Stockpiling For Disaster – The Facts You Need To Know

In this day and age, it seems as though no one should need to worry about emergencies or disasters affecting their lives. There are great security systems in place as well as lots of defenses but, unfortunately that does not guarantee safety. Terrorism from abroad isn't the only concern anymore; there are also homegrown problems and of course, Mother Nature plays a hand in history too.

No longer are people safe. The weather is changing rapidly and people's actions are now too unpredictable; and threats come in all forms.

It is just so difficult to grasp what is going to happen and even, sometimes, when you think you know, you aren't really prepared anyway. No one was really prepared for what devastation Hurricane Katrina would bring and even now, a decade later, New Orleans and its citizens are still feeling the effects.

This is just one awful example of how unpredictable disasters are, there are more, too many to count. However, if you are prepared and stockpile necessary supplies, it might just allow you to lessen the effects the disaster or emergency has on your life. Of course, your life might never be the same, but maybe, you might be able to stay alive and stay safe.

Why Do You Need To Stockpile Supplies?

In all honesty, every single person in the world should have a stockpile of groceries, medical supplies and water within their home. It's not only good sense, it's important because you may be stuck in the home or be unable to receive medical attention for a considerable period of time and you may have to rely on the items you have at hand. Without having a steady stock of supplies, you could be left with no food, no safe drinking water and no basic medical supplies either.

However, when you look at building a stockpile of items, you almost reduce the risks of being left with nothing. Now, you might think you'll be able to handle this because you have food in the cupboards and things stocked up in the refrigerator but that isn't enough. Basic food supplies can run cold in a matter of hours simply because cold foods such as deli meats, cheeses, yogurts and even frozen foods can have short expirer dates on them. These foods may allow you to survive a matter of hours but the supply line will run cold. When you use your stockpile groceries, you know there is enough to last you until the danger passes.

Another good reason why you need to start your stockpile is simply because it can be very dangerous to go outside when there is an emergency or disaster. Let's be honest, during hurricanes, tornadoes and flooding, no one generally goes outside unless they absolutely have to and even then, there aren't many. Just think for a moment how dangerous it could be to rush down to the local grocery or pharmacy to pick up supplies; you could be caught up in a storm, hurt or worst. That is why you are always advised to stay indoors.

However, if the State or city has been forewarned of a natural disaster then it sends people into a panic and goes out to panic buy. Stores generally tend to up their prices during these times, which means if you aren't prepared, you will pay out a huge amount of money for some basic supplies. Sometimes, when you try to stock up during the emergencies, you end up with items you don't need or want.

Panic buying is just crazy and unnecessary because in most cases, you'll end up paying three times more and end up fighting with a gaggle of people for the last bag of something so stupid, you'll never use. That is why you absolutely must look at stockpiling some basic supplies in your home.

The biggest reason why stockpiling is a must is due to the fact, very simply, you will be prepared for any emergency. Yes, as simple as it sounds. If you have a stockpile, you will be better prepared than 99% of the population. That is why most stockpile supplies within their home. The best thing of all is that stockpiling isn't just for minor disasters or emergencies but major ones too.

However, you aren't going to go out your way to get extra supplies but rather just stock the normal, everyday items you would buy anyway. You would opt to buy extra supplies when there is a sale on or you have extra money put aside for this but you wouldn't be purchasing stupid items that are expensive or unnecessary. Most people don't realize that many of their every day shopping items can be stockpiled for emergencies.

Is Building A Stockpile Worth The Money?

A prepper's stockpile can become one of the most valuable tools in any home today and even though money s tight, it doesn't need to stop you from creating your own stockpile. The money spent on supplies might seem a lot but actually it isn't because you can save lots of cash at every turn.

For example, if you live in an area where you often get bad weather that causes you to be unable to leave the home or make the roads dangerous to travel on, then it's a good idea to stock up with extra supplies. Buying in advance can really offer you plenty of savings.

There are plenty of everyday items you can buy in bulk at fantastic discount and savings prices. If you plan ahead, you can in fact save on petrol because you don't have to run to the shops and of course, it does save you time when you have a lazy day. OK, this isn't what stockpiles are used for but it can be useful in many ways and well worth the money too.

Buying in bulk can save you a lot of cash because while you're buying a lot of the same item, you are able to get a bulk discount. That is why most people today are choosing to buy in bulk rather than buy one-by-one. You could even use coupons when you see items you want and it's a good way to save on money too.

To be honest, the best way to build up a stockpile would be to use the seasonal savings. All year round, certain items are expensive and then suddenly go cheap or are heavily discounted after the holidays are over. Stores and shops always have surplus stock they can't sell at full price such as Easter chocolate items and Christmas foods that aren't required throughout the year. It's these items you can stock up with for very little money. Buying what's on sale can really help you make your stockpile well worth every cent spent.

In the end, building a stockpile can be excellent value even if you don't ever use it in an emergency. It's always good to have extra food stored away for a rainy day and when you add it all up, it does offer good value for money.

When Would You Need A Stockpile?

You buy extra supplies in your weekly shop, at a few dollars, and then store them away. When an emergency occurs, and can't leave the home, you have to rely on what's there in your home. For some, this is very little but for those prepared, they have an excellent stockpile of food, water and medical supplies – everything they need to stay safe during an emergency.

People ask, when will they need a stockpile, and the answer is very simple – when a disaster or emergency occurs! You never know when that is going to be but when it happens, you certainly want to know you and your family are protected and will be able to survive the upcoming days.

For example, if there is a terrible storm outside that knocks out the power and water supply, you don't have many options. You cannot leave your home because the roads might be dangerous or unsafe to travel on and everyone is being advised to stay indoors which means you have to rely on your stockpile. You will have clean and safe drinking water, foods to last you until the storm is over and medical supplies should someone be hurt. You can also have plenty of blankets to keep warm as well as lots of battery powered candles and flashlights to help keep your home lit.

Emergencies don't always come on a grand scale however, sometimes, you might have a personal emergency where you can't seek out medical treatment right away for whatever reason or might not be able to leave the home. This is when you might have to rely on your stockpiles. There could be deadly rioting going on outside or you might live in a remote area that has been cut off from food supplies. It's these times when you will need to have a stockpile ready and waiting.

Hopefully you will never need these things but is it not better to have peace of mind knowing your family is prepared than knowing they aren't?

How Much Is Enough?

This really will depend on the family home and the amount of people living within it. Now, if you are a single person or live along, it probably will be best to stock up for a few months. Usually, three months supply is enough because if you are alone when the emergency occurs, you'll be the only one consuming the food and water. You probably won't go through a huge amount in one day but ideally you want at least a three-month supply.

If you want more supplies, you can of course do so, though stocking up a three months supply would be the easiest place to start off with. You can easily put away extra foods each week to start up your supply and then you can gradually add more.

However, for families, one or two parents, the stock may very well need to be considerably bigger. The reason why is due to the fact that children tend to eat more and require more nourishment than adults. For families, small or large, it might be wise to start with a six months supply, which understandably isn't going to be easy for those on a tight budget but it's still possible to do. Even a little amount going into the stockpile fund would be helpful so that you have at least made a start, no matter how small it may seem.

Remember, coupons and special offers can really help you to start your stockpiling. Though, the amount of items you choose to stock is really down to you. Some will be comfortable with a basic month's supply while others might want to look at a six month or even a year's supply should a disaster strike.

Don't Be Afraid To Prepare

There are thousands of people right now who want to prepare for disaster and start their own little stockpile but don't because they're afraid of what people will think. It's true; there are lots of people who say prepper's are too over the top and insane; but to be honest, it isn't crazy to be prepared for the worst. Of course, you never want an emergency or disaster to strike but these things do occur and being unprepared is stupid.

It's very hard to get a realization one day tragedy could strike, but when you think about it, every high profile person is prepared. The President is prepared, Prime Ministers from around the world are prepared and even Royalty are all prepared; they have escape plans and evacuation options set up so why not do the same? You might not believe you are as important as these people but everyone is important!

The bottom line is that it is down to every individual whether or not they feel happy enough or comfortable to prepare and start stockpiling. If you aren't quite there to start, that's fine; no one is going to push you into it but if you are ready, then think about stocking up for disasters and keeping your family safe.

Chapter Two: Where to Keep Your Stockpile

Whether you have a month's supply, three month's supply or a year's supply, you can't just leave everything lying around the home. You have to choose a safe location to keep your stockpile so that the food doesn't spoil and so the home doesn't become cluttered either. However, where do you actually keep your supplies safe?

Well, you might think the kitchen cupboard is suitable but let's face it; it won't take too long to fill up. Little cupboards and shelves can easily fill up and you'll soon be looking for more space. Though, there are lots of amazing and simple storage options available to you. Really, there are hundreds of amazing little places for you to store your emergency supplies and even though your home might be on the smaller scale, it's still perfect to hold supplies.

If you have a lot of space in your home or have a considerably larger home, then it shouldn't be too difficult to find a space. You could easily use an unmanned bedroom but for smaller homes, it can be a little tricky, though not impossible. It's important to remember to keep most items together so that during an emergency, you aren't running around the home searching for supplies. Your supplies should be kept in a central location – if possible.

Organization

One thing you must have when creating a stockpile of supplies – organization! This is a must because without it, your stockpile will end up looking like a mass of junk. So, you have to gather up every item you have for your stockpile; try to bring them together in one room, the room you are using as your storage center. You can't just throw them onto shelves or into cupboards because it is going to look messy and you'll struggle to find what you need, when you need it.

This might be boring but take the time to separate each type of food stuff such as canned goods stick together and packaged items stick together. All grains should be stored together and in a dry location and the paper products such as kitchen towel and toilet paper; and handkerchiefs and tissues should also be stored together. It can seem stupid to do all this but it will help to keep things organized to a certain degree.

The next step is to clean out the area in which you are going to store the items. This means cleaning out every inch of the room and cupboards or shelves you plan to use. It is wise to do this to ensure no foods are being compromised from dirt.

Now, you must sort out the foods in terms of their expiry dates. You need to look at the sell-by dates of the food and find out what will spoil first, so which foods need to be eaten first. This should be too difficult to do and for the most part, the items you buy tend to last a while but still, always check the dates. The oldest food items should be placed at the front so they are consumed first.

Once you have sorted out the foods, you must now store the items into your cupboard and storage shelves. As you are storing the items, you should create an inventory. This is basically a list of every item you have within your supplies. You can continue to update this inventory as you buy new stock or use up old stock.

Rooms Suitable to Use to Store Your Prepper's Stockpile

You home can become a fantastic storage haven! Each and every room within your home can become a storage center. You might think your stockpile needs to be placed in or near the kitchen when in reality, that is far from the truth. If you don't have room within the kitchen or anywhere close to it, supplies can still be stored properly in other locations around the home. However, you still need to keep things in order and you need to be a little wary of where you store things too.

For most prepper's, they want to use their pantries as their first storage location. Storing supplies here can be very simple and since it's an easy access point, it's considered a central location for the home. Even if your pantry isn't particularly large, it can still be a good stockpile solution, especially if it isn't used an awful lot. However, if you have a smaller pantry, it can still be used but the storage space might become a little tight so you might need to think carefully about the pantry. You could always start a small supply storage unit here and then move elsewhere for more items, it's your choice.

The kitchen can also become a wonderful prepper's stockpile solution! You already store most of your everyday foods here anyway so it makes sense to stockpile a few extras! A room just off the kitchen can also be an excellent idea; it's a good central area and it's a room everyone can access too. Though, if you are going to store your stockpile within your kitchen, you have to remember, it's for emergencies only and not when you run out of pasta or canned fruit. The foods being stored in the kitchen that are emergency supplies are just that – for emergencies – don't be tempted to dip into them.

The garage is also another key location. It's not an area which gets heavy traffic and it's a sealed location too so there isn't much to worry about there. If you don't own a car or don't use the garage a lot then it's even better because that can be your stockpile storage room right there. Of course, you probably need to give the garage a clean out before stockpiling your items here but still, it shouldn't be too difficult. Even if you use the garage it can still be used; the supplies can be stored away in an area or corner that isn't disturbed by anyone.

Basements are good options too though you need to be wary of leaks and flooding. If you live in an area which gets flooding once or throughout a year then it's not the best location. Foods can get spoiled very easily; however, if the basement is well protected and isn't in use, then it can become a good storage option. Basements, big or small can be good storage facilities but if you're going to use the basement, make sure it's completely pest free and secured as well.

Basements and garages are probably the ideal rooms to use simply because they're often quite large and unused. Attics are also fairly good storage points too but it all depends on the type of home you have as well as whether or not the rooms are in use. If these areas are not in use or are large enough, it could be possible to build storage shelves or units that store the supplies.

Though, a bedroom and even an office or study can be used as a storage point. Of course, these areas are the least used in homes however, that doesn't mean to say you still can't use them! You can and in fact, if you have any unused or inactive rooms within a home, they can become your next stockpile and supply room! That is the great thing about your home, almost every location within it, has the potential to store anything, even emergency supplies.

For any area being used, it needs to be cleared out of any unneeded or unnecessary items as well as cleaned thoroughly too. It wouldn't be too difficult and even if there isn't much space available, you can still find room, even in a one-bedroom apartment.

Let's take one example: if you have a large walk-in closet or a closet of any kind or even an unused cupboard, these too can become storage options. Closets aren't just for clothes anymore; you can actually store your emergency stockpile supplies here, which is quite unique. However, for space, it might not offer the most but then again, it might just serve you if you plan to stock up only a month's supply. No matter the size of the stockpile supplies, they can be worthwhile and useful so even if it's quite small, it all counts.

What about living in a one bedroom home or apartment? Well, of course, the space is probably considerably limited but there are lots of options available for you. For a start, you could spread your stockpile around; this is an option for limited spaced homes. This could really give you the help to keep a stockpiled and get it up and running. Though you have to be a bit smart; I mean, you have to store foods with foods but remember they are your emergency supplies; and keep toiletries with the normal toiletries so that you aren't taking up any additional space.

Be Careful When Stockpiling In the Home

When you are stockpiling items within the home, you have to be very careful. For example, you don't want to store packaged foods in hot or humid locations or where the temperatures are likely to soar. Foods can spoil very easily when stored incorrectly and it causes you to lose a lot of money.

You need to have a safe storage point no matter where you choose to store your items. Certain things need to be avoided such as rats, rodents, insects and all manner of creatures. You also need to ensure the food is protected from the elements including excess moisture.

There are so many things that could potentially cause your stockpile to be lost. It could be anything from wrong location to insects but you have to be wary of every little problem before choosing the location of your stockpile. Yes, it's not exactly simple if you have limited space but you also have a lot of options to choose from too.

Can Anyone Stockpile?

Stocking is suitable for everyone! Anyone and everyone should consider stockpiling whether they plan for a three-day supply or a year supply; stockpiling is important. Though, you do have to be wary that this isn't going to happen overnight. Your supplies are not going to accumulate in twenty-four hours or even in a week; sometimes, it can take weeks or even longer! If you take this seriously then you could continue to add to your stockpile.

Stockpiling emergency supplies can take a matter of weeks, if not months because you cannot afford to buy everything you require in one go. Building up a stockpile could potentially cost you hundreds of dollars but do you have that all at the moment? Probably not but when you add a little piece at a time, then it is much easier and much better for you financially.

It takes serious time to build up a supply; of course, if you are just planning a three day supply then odds are, you can do this in one day. However, this is talking about serious, serious prepping and not just for minor disasters but major emergencies too. It does sound very boring but it will pay off; and remember, you aren't going to do anything you wouldn't normally do. You go off to the grocery store on your weekly shopping trip and add one or two little extras for the stockpile and that's it. There are no unnecessary trips to the supermarket, no extra waste either but even with one or two items a week, they can all add up. The cost won't seem much when disaster strikes and it is always something there to rely on too.

However, you do have to think seriously about certain things such as how long you want your supplies to last as well as what items you need. Most people make the mistake of starting their stockpile without really knowing the crucial facts and that is a waste because it costs them more time and more energy and probably more money than necessary. You have to sit down and think carefully about what foods you like and what items you will actually use also!

Once you have figured out all this then you need to start to think about how much of each item you should buy. For some, they will choose to start off with a three-day supply and that is very easy to begin with but then they continue to add to it; however, they end up with unnecessary items. What you need to do is, to think about the basic supplies first and then gage how much you'll need to stockpile.

Let's get real, you have to think about foods you're going to buy and what you're actually going to consume because if you buy several bags of rice, pasta or noodles, will you actually use them all? If not, then it's a waste of money and space. You have to come up with good ideas over what foods are suitable and it's not just foods either. Most people think supplies means food but it stretches far beyond that.

Local sales and discounts will always help to buy items but don't just buy items you don't need or will never use simply because of a discount. Grab a bargain where you can but don't buy any unnecessary items.

Store Carefully At All Times

As said above, everything needs to be stored safely especially the food items. These are the things that spoils easily though it seems most forget that. However, it doesn't actually have to be too difficult to actually store your foods because there are lots of options for you to try. You could even look at buying additional glass jars or containers that seal up so that packaged items can be stored. Plastic sealable containers work particularly well to help in the storing of foods safely and it really all just offers a little more security and peace of mind. You don't want to be stuck in an emergency and find half the stockpile has been eaten or destroyed by rodents. Getting extra storage solutions like containers or sealable jars can always help you and they are so simple to store as well which is even better.

Plastic containers and glass jars don't actually have to cost a lot either because you can recycle your old items. You can wash out old sauce jars and reuse plastic containers; recycling anything that can be sealed might be good to help with your food stored too. You can never be too careful when it comes to food.

Stockpiling Can Be Simple

If you plan to take prepping seriously then your stockpile is going to be one of your top priorities. You cannot leave anything to chance and you simply cannot compromise the safety or quality of the food either. Also, you need to look at what storage options are open to you.

You might find there are several rooms in the home suitable for storage but you need to choose one that is going to be able to hold all supplies as well as offer resistance from the changing weather. There are lots of options out there and whether or not you have particular room for a lot, having even a small stockpile can be better than having none at all.

Chapter Three: Preparing an Inventory System for Your Stockpile

How to Keep Track Of Everything within Your Stockpiles?

The first thing you must do when it comes to keeping track of your stockpile is to create an inventory system. Now, this isn't as difficult as it seems and there are lots of great options available for you to try out too. You can choose to go a little technical and create your inventory online or just stick with paper and pen – whatever suits you!

However, it would be best to set up a spreadsheet listing each item specifically, the amount of the item you have as well as its expiry date. It will be important to take stock of every item from food, to sanitary items to emergency blankets and heaters. It might seem a little extreme but actually it's really a good way to keep track.

It could be a good idea to have a physical inventory on paper and then a second inventory stored digitally on your computer. The digital inventory will be much easier to change than paper and this can be taken with you at any location and it can even be stored on your cell phone too.

Stay Organized To Help Rotate Old Items

From time-to-time you will have to rotate the items you have. Foods will go off and things such as clothing might need to be replaced when you lose or gain weight. It can be so easily done however when you have a good routine set out.

For example, at the end of every month, you should go to the supply area and look through the foods to check on the expiry dates. If you see any that are nearing their expiry dates, it's time to remove them from the supplies and eat them or thrown them away, whichever you prefer. Ideally, you don't want to waste food.

However, it is going to be important to keep a close eye on every item within the stock and continue to check on the food, clothing, and the condition of the batteries to ensure they still have full power. This can be done once a month or even once every two months.

Don't Forget To Replace Items with New Ones

As old stock is removed from the supplies, you can easily forget to replace it. Now, this is easily done because you might remember on Monday but by Friday when you do the weekly grocery shop, you could end up forgetting. This means the supplies are down by one or possibly several items and if you forget to replenish them, soon there will be hardly anything left.

You must remember to replace whatever reaches its expiry date so that the stocks remain at full strength. You should actually think about consuming some parts of the stockpile when the foods are about to expire and then rotate the other items and of course restock what you've eaten so that it remains at full capacity.

Chapter Four: Items You Need For Your Stockpile

Emergencies occur at the least expected of times and you always must remain prepared. Whether you live in a hurricane alley or just face a crisis, the items you have within your stockpile supplies might just end up saving your life. However, everyone knows that food and water are the key elements but what foods should be taken and what other items are necessary to have?

Foods Suitable For Stockpiling

Everyone has their own likes, dislikes and tastes so while most people have a specific idea in mind, it will be important to stick with some of the basic items. Canned fruit is always a sure-fire winner because most people enjoy fruit and that can last such a long period of time too, which makes it perfect! Canned goods are always great to have though; you should stick with the foods that are sure to be consumed!

Sardines and tuna are probably good seafood to opt for but most others are not simply because you can buy tuna and sardines in tin form. Smoked salmon and cod are often found fresh or frozen and these aren't good to stockpile. Tinned fish is much better and lasts a lot longer too.

Condensed and powdered milk might not be the most appealing of milk options out there but they aren't terrible options either. They do tend to have a good shelf life and they are so simple to make too; in fact, a lot of foods today contain condensed and powdered milk anyway! Soy and rice milk can be good alternatives to consider too.

Soups are usually good and since they come in packet form and can form, you have two options. You can easily stock up with your favorite flavors and let's be honest; you can't go wrong with soup can you? Though packet soups might be a bit of a hit or miss because, if they need water, you'll need to dig into your water supply; it shouldn't be a big hit.

Pasta and pasta sauces; these items are usually very good to take along with you simply because they are easy to cook and don't require a lot of shelf space. Canned stews and chili can do the trick too and peanut butter, you can't forget this. However, for jams and jellies, they can be a bit of a hit and miss too simply because their expiry dates are long lasting but if store incorrectly can go off quickly. If you see any mold on these items, discard; you can of course stick with a small supply of jams and jellies but don't go too over the top.

Beans and canned vegetables are always a winner because you can't go wrong with them. Don't forget to look for some of these while at the grocery store. Crackers, beef jerky, cereal, packages nuts, granola and granola bars are great items to have too. They are dried foods but they can be opened and eaten immediately and perfect for having to eat while on the go.

Packaged items that require water to cook them can still be good, though they are not the best foods to take with you when you have to leave quickly. The reason why is because having to carry extra cooking equipment isn't always good. Though, packages items for the home are great; you only have to use a little bit of water to cook them. Things such as noodles, tea, and hot chocolate, coffee and instant pasta are good to stick with.

For drinks, you have a variety of options available to you. Of course, you are going to start with water and you should have a good few gallons of this within your home but it's not the only beverage option. Carton and canned juices are perfect for stocking up because they generally have long expiry dates and usually taste descent. It's the same with sports drinks, although some of these drinks can be a little more costly than canned but it varies. You should have maybe a week's supply of sports or energy drinks simply because these probably will be used once or twice in a week so they last longer.

Medical Supplies to Consider
Firstly, you need to start with the basics of medical items you'll likely need. Bandages, sterile hand-wash, plasters or band-aids, antimicrobial gel to clean cuts and wounds; and gauze and strapping

for broken bones. These are the basic of items you are going to need for your first aid kit; now, you can assemble one of opt to buy a full first aid kit from the stores.

However, you also need to think about stockpiling important over-the-counter medicines for common colds. You may want to look at painkillers, medicines that allow you to keep colds or fevers at bay; throat medications for sore throats. Allergy medications are also important to have should there suddenly be an allergy attack.

It is also important to ensure you have a full prescription on hand whenever you need it. If you are on any long-term medication, it will be important to have a full prescription with you at all times and maybe even a spare prescription with the stockpile. The reason why is simply because if you are stuck in the home for a long period of time and cannot get medical help, the medication is there for you.

The most serious of prepper's tend to stockpile surgery items and even vaccines but let's be totally honest; you might not need these things. Of course, you can't know what's around the corner but these items are often difficult to find and expensive to buy. Sometimes, they aren't going to be needed and you have to think logically. I'm not going to sit and list vaccines because it is very unlikely you'll get your hands on any so let's just stick to what you can actually use.

Sanitation, Hygiene and Power Supplies

Toilet tissue and wipes are not the only items needed for proper hygiene; you will also need soap, new diapers as well as ways to dispose of these things. If you cannot get out of the home, then it is going to be tricky but not impossible. For hygiene, try and use a diaper changer to store diapers or for ladies personal sanitation items, they should be wrapped up in little bags and put into a trashcan.

However, to help keep away animals and to reduce the smell, try and cover them with additional garbage bags and keep them locked away in a cupboard so that it doesn't disrupt your household too much. This isn't ideal but if you cannot get out of the home, it's one of the options available.

Also, for women's personal hygiene and sanitation products, every lady knows what this means, she should have a stockpile of necessary items. Every lady is different but they will know what they need; and it might be a good idea to have a three or four month's supply at the very least.

Power supplies are not always going to be the easiest of issues to prepare for however, you can still prepare yourself. Back-up power sources are always good to help get juice back into the home, even if it's only for a few hours or days; every little helps in emergencies. Also, if you have electricity still, you may want to conserve it by switching off unnecessary power outlets.

However, if you find yourself with no electricity whatsoever and no generator for back-up power, then it's time to go back to basics. You need to rely on flashlights and candles and while some candles are always safe, you can rely on battery-powered candles. Now, battery powered candles can last a good amount of time and run off batteries which means one less issue to worry about. Tea lights are great to offer more power even though it's not the best.

What Else Do You Need?

It seems obvious but a lot of people don't keep a can opener in their home. However, if you are stockpiling canned goods, you need to have two! You want a back-up can opener so that if something goes wrong or you accidently break or lose the first, there is always a second one to rely on. It's the same with batteries, you should always have a good stock and supply of batteries in all shapes and sizes because different items require different batteries.

Pet food is always important if you own a pet. You don't want them to go hungry either and you can't have them munching in on your supplies either. The dogs, cats, fish, hamsters, rabbits and every other pet needs to have their own little supply so that if there is an emergency they are able to get food.

A hunting knife can be good but only when you are actually planning to do some hunting. If you are caught outdoors during a disaster, then a hunting knife can help to provide you with nourishment from wild animals.

Keeping the Family Safe

Only you know whether or not you are going to choose to arm yourself. If you are, then you must know how to safely use the weapon you have as well as sure how to store it safely. For example, if you were to choose to arm your home with a small handgun or pistol, you should know how to keep it clean and in good shape as well as how to carefully store this too.

If you plan not to arm yourself with a weapon, you should also stock up with supplies to help guard the home such as extra nails and wood to board up the home. However, everyone has their own opinion on this. For those who choose to arm themselves, they need to have a fair supply of ammunition but don't go overboard.

Chapter Four: Useful Things to Barter With and Tips and Tricks for You to Try

Bartering has become one of the oldest tools of the trade throughout the world. People have bartered for hundreds of years and will continue to do so and you must learn to barter if you want to boost your stockpile and get much-needed supplies during a crisis. While you can be prepared, you can only prepare so much and there may come a time when you have to barter in order to gain something valuable.

Water Purification Supplies, Alcohol and Water

To be honest, anything can be bartered for anything in today's world but let's just stick to disasters and emergencies. This is the time when people can barter for all sorts of crazy things and you need to know what people are going to be looking for.

Water, water purification supplies and alcohol are three of the biggest bargaining tools during a crisis. The reason why – well, you can't have too much water; and you might not have any water purification supplies to keep your water supply suitable. Of course, alcohol might not seem necessary but many people can use this during a crisis and if you have plenty of it, why not use it to barter for something more useful?

You could actually look to exchange water or alcohol for medical supplies or extra food or whatever you were low on. Remember, water is the most bartered for item in the world because without it, you couldn't survive and during a crisis, a lot of people find themselves short of water. If you find you have an excess water supply, you could actually look to barter some with items you need. Of course, this doesn't mean giving away your entire supply but just a small portion for necessary items.

However, hand tools, first aid kits, batteries, matches, lighters, sanitary products, fuel, antibiotics and painkillers are all good bartering tools to work with. It doesn't matter if you need these products or want to use them to barter with; you can use them to your advantage. Most people are willing to barter if they need additional supplies and you could do this too.

Look For Equal Bartering

When you barter however, you shouldn't be left with the bad end of a deal because it will be you left with the problems. One of the biggest tricks and tips to be wary of is ensuring the deal you make is going to be one of equal portions. You have to go into the deal with an open mind and know what you are getting for your exchange.

For example, if you were bartering or trading a two-gallon bottle of water as well as a pack of batteries and all you were getting was a tin of tuna, it's not a fair deal. You absolutely need to set out what you are willing to give and what the other person is willing to give also. It doesn't matter if you are the one who wants to barter water for food or vice versa because both parties must get an equal deal.

If you don't make an equal deal there is no one left to blame apart from yourself!

Barter For What You Need and Nothing More

You are bartering for a reason – you need to trade for something important – but do not make the mistake of believing you need more than what is necessary. A lot of people during emergencies, especially when they've been forced to bug out of their home, end up bartering much needed supplies for things they really done need. It is not just a waste but it could cost you dearly!

It's like stockpiling food; you only stock what you know you will need and what you will use. If you go on a crazy bartering spree, you'll end up with nothing and be in a worse position than ever before.

Stay Safe and Know What the Deal Is

Before making any sort of a deal, ensure you will be safe. This isn't always easy to do especially during a crisis but you have to meet somewhere that is relatively safe such as a community center. Meeting out in the middle of nowhere could be dangerous and deadly. Also, you have to understand what you are getting for the trade and what you are willing to trade.

Do not trade anything you are not comfortable with and if in doubt, think twice. Don't be afraid to say no and if unsure, ask for clarification.

Think Of All Goods You No Longer Need

Let's say you had a full gas can but you were forced to leave the car because it broke down or run into a ditch. You probably will be on foot for the rest of the journey but you have an extra can of gas you don't need. There isn't much you can do with this especially if the car is gone; however, you could use this to your advantage because you can exchange this for a ride to safety.

If someone has enough room in their vehicle, they might be willing to take you along with them if you offer them the gas. It's the same with items you have you don't actually need; you might be able to barter with someone for them to help you out.

Stay Wary

No matter where you choose to make the deal or what you choose to barter with, you always need to keep yourself safe first. Being wary to your surroundings allows you to stay one step ahead of the game. You can avoid dangerous situations and when a successful barter transaction has been complete, you can go on your way safely.

Chapter Five: How and Why To Start Building Your Stockpile Now

A true prepper will know the importance of setting up the best stockpile they possibly can but what happens if you aren't prepared yet? Newcomers often find themselves a little stuck and a little unsure of where to turn to because there is so much information out there telling them all sorts.

Many newbie's are a little afraid when they hear people talk about end-of-the-world stuff too but don't be frightened and don't be confused either! Learning how to start building your stockpile can be very simple and easy to do and remember every prepper started where you are starting – at the bottom!

Starting from the very beginning might seem daunting but actually it's not. Building your stockpile can be easy and a little fun when you make it! You don't have to do anything fancy and you really are going to do your normal, everyday tasks with maybe one or two minor exceptions – but nothing strenuous!

Plan out Your Stockpile List

First and foremost, every prepper's stockpile must start off with a list. Now while this might seem a little boring, it's actually important because if you just go off buying anything at random, you'll end up with items you don't need. So, start off with a pen and paper and start listing the items you will need; go for the basics first and then work your way to other so-called luxury items.

It might be best to take a walkthrough of the refrigerator as well as the kitchen cupboards to establish the type of items you already consume. Make notes of what products you eat such as fish, pasta, and cheese and once you have listed a variety of foods, go back through the list. You are going to have items and products on there that won't last through a certain period of time.

For example, dairy products like cheese, eggs, butter and spreads are not going to last more than a few days at best before they shouldn't be consumed which means they need to be removed from the list. However, things such as pasta, toilet tissue, shampoo, soap and batteries, they are all items that are long-lasting and are priorities.

It's important to stick with foods you know everyone loves and know won't waste if the power goes off. When you have removed inappropriate items, you'll be left with a list that is suitable to help you stockpile. Of course, luxury items such as chocolate and candies can be purchased but other items should be purchased before them! You won't need to have bubble bath are similar unnecessary items. When you have a list, you will start to purchase the items you need and no more. This will help you avoid crazy purchases because if you don't need them, don't buy them!

Temptation will be there in the shops but when you're buying supplies, stick to the list! If you really have to buy something then keep it in your regular food cupboard and don't mix it up with supplies.

Understand How Much Bottled Water You Need

Water is a vital source for anyone and you have to be able to gage the amount you'll need during a crisis. This is never easy but having a good stockpile of this will be important. Now, having several gallon of water stored within the home might seem a little extreme but actually it's not, because you can never tell when the water supply will be interrupted. You might find your home if left without proper water supply for the next week or possibly longer; during severe flooding, it can leave the home without clean water for months.

Emergencies bring out all sorts of trouble and being able to source water is one of the hardest problems for people today, even for those who are prepared. That is why it's important to store a good amount of water within the home. Though, buying water in bulk will be more cost effective than buying bottle by bottle.

In fact, you should have a supply of bottled water to drink and cook with as well as have a second supply of water for washing with. Sometimes, if there are severe problems outside with storms or violent weather, the water supply coming into your home might be disrupted for a lengthy period of time.

Think About Additional Items Such As Household Items

Food and water are the first thoughts for most people when they look at stockpiling up supplies for emergencies and disasters but they aren't the only things important. You also need to think about having enough blankets within the home to stay warm, alternative heating options, sanitation and lots of other factors. These are just as important as food and water and you really need to also concentrate on these items.

Be Organized While Shopping

You must be organized when it comes to keeping on top of your stockpile supplies. You simply cannot go around the grocery store or supermarket throwing in anything you like because it's on offer or because you think it'll get used. This is a good way to waste money and that is not what you want, especially if you are working with a household budget. It doesn't matter if your budget is relatively small or large, you must have a workable budget and that unfortunately means planning out your strategy.

You really do need to have some sort of plan of attack or strategy whilst out shopping. When you create your weekly shopping list, ensure you add a few additional items that are solely for the stockpile supplies. You can even set out a small budget for these additional items such as five dollars, maybe less; it doesn't matter but you do need to stay organized otherwise its sheer chaos.

Watch Out For Sales and Discounts

When you want to create your stockpile successfully, you always must look at the savings you make. For a start, stores have massive clear outs during the year before the new line comes out; and after holidays, sales come in abundance and this is the time for you to strike. You need to head on over to the shops when you hear of massive reductions and discounts because it's the chance to stockpile and save cash.

This works for food, toiletries and even clothes! In fact, clothes are especially good to buy when on discount because it usually means the store is looking to get rid of their excess surplus before the new season items arrives which gives you time to stock up for less. Now, for warmer clothes, look just before the Fall or Summer lines come out because this is the time when stores are looking to ditch old stock and make room for new garments. You can stock up on woolly socks, thermals and garments you will need if the power supply shuts off. As long as it fits and keeps you warm, it's worth buying especially when marked down to basically nothing.

Closing down sales is especially good for picking up a bargain or two. Stores who are unfortunately going out of business will try and sell their stock as cheaply as possible and it's here where you can pick up a lot of bargains. Though, if you don't need whatever they have on offer, don't buy; and it's the same if the prices are steep – don't buy. Only make a purchase if you think you're getting a good deal for your money, otherwise, walk away. Though, you do have to be a bit wary and try on the clothing before purchasing because with closing down sales, if you buy and try to return them later, you might not be able to.

Bulk buying is great too for those who want to get a head start on their supplies. You can end up saving anything from twenty percent to sixty, or sometimes even more. It all depends on what you're buying of course and where you source your stock too. However, buying in bulk seems to be a firm favorite for many today especially when it offers them a great discount.

Shop Wary

Everyone is different in their approach to prepping their stockpile and sometimes, it isn't all going to be housed in one room. For space issues, it isn't going to be logical to shop without really first working out what sort of space you're working with. Let's take an example; if you were looking to buy a month's supply of pasta or rice, do you have space for all this? What is more, is it going to be needed? You have to really think first before you shop!

The basics need to be concentrated on first because other items are worried about. Also, it might mean having to stock your supplies in a variety of locations throughout the home. This means, you also have to think about how easily it will be to store certain items. You can't ideally have a three-month's supply of rice if it takes up most of your storage space.

Too many preppers' don't shop wary and end up with an overflowing house full of items they are never going to need or use. It's best to stick with a small supply at first and dot it around the house if space is an issue and then when more space becomes available, use it for your supplies. However, it's not a wise move to go out and shop for unnecessary items.

Keep the Food Eatable

You probably already have the idea that cheese, eggs and most other dairy products are not going to be on your stockpile shopping list but that doesn't mean other foods are easy to store either. Everything has its own storage needs and you must think about how you are actually going to store the foods. Some can't be in direct sunlight and others need to be kept in a dry, cool place.

It's simple things such as these that can harm your stockpile efforts, so be wary. Check out how to store the foods you plan to buy first and then store them correctly. In most cases, packaged and canned goods need to be stored in dry and cool places, away from direct sunlight. For example, if you plan to use a basement or garage, that would be perfect. However, don't be fooled, always double check before storing any item.

Understand Your Items

To be honest, some items that are suitable for stocking can go out of date eventually and you must be aware to that fact. You need to research how long it is safe to keep certain goods for before they need to be thrown away; even with canned goods, they have expiry dates too so don't think they will last forever because they don't. In most cases, the stockpile foods you choose probably will have long lasting dates but it's still good to check; you might find one or two items at the store that don't have long dates on them and if that's the case, look elsewhere.

Ideally your foods are going to last a long time; it's the same with batteries. You want to ensure they are completely new and are good to last until you need them. Long shelf life items are always the things you want to look at first. They might cost you a little in the beginning but once you get your stockpile up and running, they won't cost much.

Don't Always Stick To Big Name Brands

If you are really struggling with money and have to make savings, despite you looking to stockpile, you can always switch brands. Now in many cases, there isn't much difference between the big named brands and the lesser-known brands. This might be an avenue for you to explore when it comes to saving cash because some brands which are less recognized might be cheaper.

Of course, before you buy any new brands that are cheaper, you should try them out first to ensure you and your family like them. However, if you do, you can always look at the smaller brands to help you save money and still build your stockpile.

Though, if you really aren't enjoying different brands, you should look at buying the bigger named brands only when they are on special offer. This will help save a little money and get the important goods for the stockpile.

Forget the Perishables

Sometimes, you can freeze perishables and store them for a while but if you don't use them, they can be a waste. Do you really have money to waste? No, of course not and you shouldn't waste money either! It might be worth ditching perishables for the emergency supplies and concentrate on items that are long lasting instead.

Cheeses and dairy products are all something we enjoy but they don't always last long, even when stored carefully. It might be wise to save money for your supplies by avoiding dairy. For regular shopping, go nuts but for emergency supplies, be sensible.

Look For Seasonal Savings

When you really want to improve your stockpile and emergency supplies, you are best to go off on a shopping spread during the seasonal sales. Now, you can pick up a few items for the supplies during Christmas, Thanksgiving, New Year, Easter and the 4th of July but it's much easier to find deals after they are over.

When its New Year week, stores are still going to sell Christmas Puddings and seasonal foods and it may very well be the time for you to pick up some good deals. Sometimes, weeks after the holidays are long over, stores are left with excess stock they need to get rid of and it's the time to get great deals. You never know, you might be able to pick up a hamper full of goodies for a fraction of the original price, if not cheaper!

Why Start Today?

There has never been a better time to get out there and start gathering your stockpile supplies! You could put it off until week or next month but will there ever be a time for you to start? Of course, you'll put it off until it's too late.

You really never know when an emergency, crisis or disaster is going to strike and if you're unprepared, you put your life at risk even more so then when prepared. However, by stating up a simple stockpile of basic supplies such as food, water, medicine and blankets, you can almost give yourself and your family the best chance to ride out the storm.

This is why more and more people are choosing to stockpile than ever before! It's as simple as that and since the world is unpredictable, it's one of the biggest reasons why prepping a stockpile is necessary.

Conclusion

Prepping your stockpile isn't as difficult as you might believe; there are so many simple but effective ways to start. You don't have to be a pro or have a lot of cash either, you can start off with a three day supply and then work your way from there – it's that easy!

Good luck, fellow preppers!

*****

Prepping Hacks: Beginner Tips to Survive Almost Anything

What is prepping and who is it for? Prepping is a desire to succeed in and be prepared for a survival situation, ranging from natural disasters to economic collapse and any other unfortunate event – even zombies. Stocking up on food, medicine and survival gear is your insurance against tragedy. Regardless of your level of disposable income or living situation, you can definitely take steps to protect yourself from disaster – prepping is for EVERYONE.

How do we begin to cover this vast topic and all there is to consider? It can seem overwhelming, that's for sure. That's why we're cutting straight to the chase with this book: Prepping Hacks. These are the things you can start on right now, today.

The most important thing you can do to protect yourself, your property and your loved ones is to just start. Purchase and store what you can. Most folks are not made of money and living on acres, but just by starting to prepare and think like a prepper will put you light years ahead of someone with more resources but no concern for entertaining the idea of a survival situation.

On a Budget?

No matter who you are, you have a budget. A budget of time, space and money – there's never enough, is there? How can you consider yourself a prepper when you can't afford an AR-15? What if you don't have room to store giant barrels of grain like the guy you saw on TV? And who has the time to learn how to craft their own bullets? When you prepare for a survival situation, you are hoping to *survive* the event.

You can't and you won't have every conceivable survival supply item on the market. There really aren't any set standards or requirements for you to meet, and any steps you take are better than none. Any thought that you've given a possible scenario will help you far more than any gadget. Indeed, there are many gadgets and gizmos out there which are specifically marketed towards preppers in hopes of cashing in on this craze.

It's up to you to evaluate what is truly useful for your particular situation, and discover when there are cheaper alternatives that can still get the job done. You don't need anything fancy, you just need something that *works*. So, you don't have room for a man-sized gun safe? You probably don't need one, either. Focus on filling up the little spaces in your apartment with nonperishable food and water.

Maybe you've got some spots left under the bed, or you could add shelf space to your laundry room. If you don't have a lot of time, that's fine. Use your time *wisely*. Read about prepping and search the internet for tips, advice and hacks to make your life easier. It's okay to be busy, prepping doesn't *have* to be a fulltime commitment. It's a lifelong endeavor, where you can watch your skills and supplies build slowly over time.

You probably wanted to start prepping to calm some anxiety about a possible doomsday scenario. Let's not also accumulate anxiety over how your preps measure up, as well.

Bugging In or Out

Depending on the situation you find yourself in, it may be safer to remain in your home or you may have to abandon it. This is the choice between bugging in and bugging out. Bugging in might be a much more appealing and comfortable proposition. You will be surrounded by all your belongings, a comfortable bed, changes of clothes and four walls to protect you. In this space, you enjoy your family photo albums, houseplants and hobbies.

You are comforted by your familiarity with the area and the deadbolt on the front door. Who wouldn't want to remain in the comfort of their own home? Leaving it all behind is probably the *last* thing anyone would want to do. But there may come a time where it is unwise or even deadly to shelter in place. What if there were approaching wildfires? What if a viral outbreak spread far and wide throughout your community inducing riots and pandemonium?

You might even be doing just fine at home, but you have run out of food and need to scavenge an ever expanding area. You may have ridden out the apocalypse, but things have gotten so bad that you must head out to find survivors to help rebuild society. If things get too heated, you may have to bug out – preferably to a secondary location previously decided upon.

Bugging out could mean leaving in your vehicle, but many disaster scenarios could bring traffic to a standstill. There is always the possibility that you will have to escape on foot, off the beaten path away from other people. Bugging out means you will be preparing to think on your feet and live off the land, as seen in so many survivor shows on television.

Sometimes you can pick up some great advice from these programs, but at the end of the day the hosts still have camera crews and medics following them around. Surviving in the outdoors is not something to be taken lightly. Try it out for a few days if you can. Head out for an extended camping session with your bugout bag and practice the survival techniques you picked up.

Something as essential as building a fire or a shelter is a lot more work than people realize. If you cannot reliably provide yourself with food, shelter and water for at least 3 days, you know that you have some work to do. Be sure to study survival manuals and outdoor guides, just in case you're ever forced into the wilderness.

Threat Levels

When it hits the fan, and you are ready to tough it out, your actions will widely be determined by the threat level you are facing. When there's a bad thunderstorm outside, we might tune in to weather alerts, grab a few candles and stay away from the windows. And yeah, if a giant herd of walking dead was lumbering down your street you might want to grab your bag and your shotgun and get the heck out, heading for an unpopulated area.

The duration of these events are going to be different. You can ride out the storm for the night, and if the fabled zombies infect enough people you may be on the run for months or even years. An event with minimal impact and short duration will have you reacting differently than a severe threat that will require self-reliance for an extended period of time.

Any citizen, at the very least, should have enough supplies to see them through the immediate crisis of a minimal event and possibly three to five days after. Any budget should allow you to stow away some extra food and water. You don't need anything fancy or expensive, you are covering the bare necessities like sustenance and hygiene.

Once you have collected enough items for a minimal event, by all means add to it as resources allow. Grow your stockpiles and invest in survival gear little by little while you consider a more severe event. Primary items that follow are bare necessities that everyone should have to be prepared for a minimal event.

Make sure you have this list covered first, then move on to secondary items as you are able to afford them, securing your future when things get really grim.

Food for Preppers

Your main concern when prepping should be cultivating your stockpiles of nonperishable food and water. Even if you have very little to spend, you can still start small and simply add an item or two when grocery shopping to put away for hard times. Having extra items in the pantry that will keep for months or even years is always a smart investment, as you can fall back on your extra supplies in the event of a job loss or unexpected expense.

This makes prepping even more relevant to those who have little in the way of disposable income. If you do seem to have more time than money, you could certainly try your hand at canning/preserving foods at home as well. It is relatively inexpensive to start with and can help you take full advantage of the bounty of your garden or the frugality of buying in bulk. Make sure as your stockpile grows that you check expiration dates and rotate items to be consumed first to the front of your storage.

You'll only have to do this about every three months as long as you save items with a shelf life *longer* than that. The best way to extend the shelf life beyond the suggested "use by" date is to store food in cool temperatures away from sunlight. There are lots of items available that keep for a really long time, and they often end up being some of the cheapest! Most of the suggested foods that follow are ideal for tossing in the trusty bugout bag as well, just be sure to select ones that are lightweight and preferably ready to eat.

- Rice
- Beans
- Potatoes
- Matzo bread
- Canned seafood like tuna, sardines, salmon, trout and even octopus
- Bottled water
- Applesauce
- Granola bars
- Nuts
- Canned vegetables like green beans, corn and tomatoes
- Canned fruits like peaches, pineapple and fruit cocktail
- Hearty canned soups that don't require additional water
- Juice boxes
- Fruit snacks
- Beef jerky and beef sticks
- Honey
- Peanut butter singles
- Canned cheese
- Canned chicken
- Instant mashed potatoes
- Evaporated milk

- Dried fruit such as raisins, banana chips, apricots and prunes
- Fruit preserves
- Fruit leather
- Saltines
- Spam
- Graham crackers

Hygiene and Medical Care

No matter how careful you are in your day to day life, you will occasionally get sick or suffer a minor injury. And that's fine as long as you can pick up medicine at the store and visit the doctor when you need help. But during an emergency or an extended crisis your options become limited. You're going to have to play doctor now.

It is widely recommended to have a basic medical kit in your home kept for emergencies, and you can even buy preassembled kits in a vast range of sizes. These are handy because they are self-contained and you can grab it when you need it and have everything at hand. Most likely one of these would be sufficient to get you through a short lived disaster in which you are bugging in at home. But there may be other items you would like to add to your kit if you have certain medical conditions, or for the possibility of having to bug out.

If you are planning on being self-reliant for the long haul, carefully consider how you would handle a more serious injury. Treating broken limbs, deep lacerations or even gunshot wounds are not within the parameters of your little drugstore kit. There are other kits available out there which are based on military grade medical supplies. You will most likely have to search online for one of these, and they are definitely a little more expensive.

Even buying one of these may not cover everything you personally need. What you *should* do is review all the supplies available to you and customize a list to suit your needs. The items listed are simple suggestions to help you determine what should be in your home kit and your bugout bag.

- Ibuprofen- relieves pain, swelling *and* fevers
- Antibacterial ointment- keep your cuts and sores *clean*
- Bandages in various sizes
- Gauze, medical tape and scissors
- Fabric bandage for sprains- you have to stay mobile when you bugout
- Splint- fractured limbs need to be immobilized
- Hydrocortisone- an anti-itch cream can save you from bug bites, poison ivy and all kinds of skin rashes and allergic reactions

- Aloe and sunscreen- bugging out means you're going to be in the sun, you can even get a sunburn in winter conditions, so protect yourself when possible
- Tweezers- you may find a nasty splinter or a pesky wood tick
- Antibacterial wipes or hand sanitizer- whatever you're doing, try to keep clean
- Antidiarrheal medication- think about *this* when you're living in the woods
- Antacids and anti-gas capsules- these are simply to ease discomfort, but keeping comfortable can improve morale
- Aspirin- pain reliever commonly used for people at risk of heart attacks
- Antifungal cream- just in case all your hard, sweaty work leads to athlete's foot or jock itch, fungus is *not* going to go away on its own
- Hot shower bag- check these out for a super cool camping accessory, definitely will improve morale and hygiene
- Bleach tablets and iodine- can help purify water and sanitize instruments
- Tourniquet- you've got to stop the bleeding if you want to keep your people
- Hydrogen peroxide- can be used to flush out wounds or as mouthwash

- Garlic is famous for its antibacterial and antimicrobial properties, can cure colds when ingested – you can even apply it topically or near an infected area
- Vitamins
- Animal antibiotics- fish antibiotics include penicillin, amoxicillin and clindamycin which is helpful if you learn the proper dosages
- Prednisone may be helpful to reduce allergic reactions such as inflammation, but it is tricky figuring out how to begin doses and taper them off

- Sleep aids- to be used with caution
- N95 face masks- filters out particles in the air, can even help with seasonal allergies
- Feminine products
- Toothpaste, toothbrush and floss
- Bucket with a toilet lid and lots of plastic bags
- Extra pair of prescription lenses
- Extra prescribed medications

Remember that expiration dates on medication are only the guarantee the manufacturer wants to uphold, and almost all medicines aside from liquids and those requiring refrigeration can last two to five years with almost full potency. You can safely stockpile more medicine than you can use up in a year, as long as you rotate your stock and use up the oldest items first.

<u>Your Bugout Bag</u>

Every prepper needs to have a bugout bag, also called a go bag or 72 hour bag. The purpose of your bugout bag is to have enough supplies to live off of for at least three days in a pre-packed bag that you can just grab and go. If things aren't safe at home anymore, you should be able to just drop everything and rely on the backpack you placed by the door.

Everyone's bag is different, as everyone's needs and environment are different. When you pack your supplies, consider the climate, terrain and your target destination. When you're on your own, your mission is to secure food, water and shelter. Most people bring too much stuff, and exceed the amount they can comfortably carry.

The rule of thumb is to keep your bag to 25% of your total body weight, and that is if you are generally healthy and fit. Hiking for a few miles with your bag will tell you if it's too heavy, in which case you will have to remove some items or replace them with lighter ones. There are many ultralight items which are being made to serve this purpose, as well as tools that combine several items into one.

So whether you have a military knapsack, mountaineering bag or a plain old backpack, test its weight and keep improving it as you go. Many times there's something you really want to bring, but it's not considered essential for life. If you are with other people, everyone can carry a few different specialized items, as you will only need one for the entire group. In the end,, it's all up to you when you pack your bugout bag. The items that follow are main essentials for surviving outside the home, and you will decide to add or delete items as you go.

- A few snacks, like granola bars, beef jerky or trail mix
- A full water bottle with an included filter
- Nonperishable items such as canned goods or MRE's (meals ready to eat)
- Small metal cup or pot for cooking and collecting water
- Ultralight sleeping bag or bedroll
- Reflective emergency blanket
- Plastic sheeting, duct tape and rope or paracord for shelter, or an ultralight tent
- Two ways of making fire, such as a lighter, waterproof matches and a flint striker
- Compass and map of surrounding area
- Basic medical kit
- High quality survival knife
- Handgun and extra ammunition
- A change of clothes
- Multi-tool with can opener
- Signaling mirror or flares
- Hand sanitizer and cleansing cloths

- Toilet paper, to use sparingly
- Rain poncho can be used to keep you or your pack dry
- Flashlight, either handheld or worn on the head
- Several baggies to keep small items safe and dry

A Word on Knives

You're not going to get far in any survival situation without a good knife. A knife is by far the most useful and versatile tool available, and this is why many people carry a small pocket knife with them everywhere they go. Aside from violence, which may be necessary in an act of self-defense, a knife can provide you with a means of cutting, splitting, prying or even digging. Any knife is better than none, but while we're out shopping, what all needs to be considered?

First, let's examine the difference between a folding blade and a fixed blade. A folding blade is small and easy to carry, you can comfortably bring a means of survival with you every day, wherever you go. Go for a Swiss Army style, with all of its attachments, and you're ready for anything. Small odd jobs can be accomplished with your folding blade, no worries. But a blade that folds is weaker, and can't hold up to heavy duty tasks or battle.

The joint in the folding blade is a weak spot that will eventually give and break. A fixed blade is one piece of metal that will absorb energy evenly and is far more durable. If you're aiming to cut through wood or stab an attacker, you'll need the reliability of a fixed blade. Since they don't fold, they take up more space and should be carried in an appropriate sheath. Perhaps it's best to keep a folding blade in your pocket and bugout bag, while relying on your fixed blade when you need something more stable – or threatening.

The other factor in the strength of your knife is the *tang* – the length of the actual piece of metal the blade is constructed from. A full tang blade will reach past the hilt and all the way down the handle, and this is definitely what you should be looking for. If your blade stops where the handle starts or tapers off into the handle, it will eventually break. Like the joint in a folding knife, the point where the metal ends creates a weak spot. If you see a pretty knife and it's on the cheaper side, determine whether it is full tang or not. If not, you may need to keep looking.

For functionality and ease of use, choose a knife that ends in a sharp, *pointed* tip. There are many different shapes for blade edges and ends, but what you as a *prepper* are looking for is reliability, not style. If you need to cut or stab into something, a pointed end will be the easiest to pull back out. Serrations, holes and curves can increase the likelihood of your knife becoming lodged in your target, and you may need your knife back!

Choosing a knife with a pointed tip will aid you in many survival tasks, such as picking at a splinter or loosening a screw when you have no other tools at your disposal. You can purchase and carry as many different blade styles as you like, but make sure you have a sharp point on your most prized and trusted knife.

Weapons Ready

Whether you like it or not, there may come a time when you need to defend yourself from a deadly attack. Despite your best efforts to fly under the radar and secure your perimeter, you now have a violent intruder breaking into your home. What will you do now?

In a prolonged survival situation, hiding may not be enough and you may have to fight to stay alive. The threat will come with no regard for your law abiding, peaceful nature – and you're not going to be able to negotiate with a bear in your campsite or a zombie on your lawn. You *must* arm yourself to survive, even if you tell yourself you'll never raise your weapon. Fine. Don't. But how about you bring a weapon along just in case you change your mind?

Firearms

Having a gun at the ready during your worst nightmare scenario can really improve your odds of survival. If someone is set on threatening your right to survive, just point and shoot, like a camera! It really is terrible that such a weapon exists that can take a person off this planet so easily and thoughtlessly.

But we are preparing for a prolonged disaster, where people will take the law into their own hands – it's best you have a weapon like a firearm to quickly get you out of danger if the situation really does call for it. You don't need a million guns, just one or two would do nicely. In reality you don't need more guns than you have people to fire them. If you want to stockpile something, amass large quantities of ammo for your weapons.

Keeping your chosen firearms in only a few calibers will keep things simple for the people utilizing your armory. If you just appreciate guns and fancy yourself a collector, go ahead and explore your passion, but decide on allocating certain purchases for use when it really does hit the fan.

Handguns – Many people simply keep a handgun in the home just in case someone breaks in at night, and this is a good place to start. All handguns are easily carried and operated, and are definitely lethal, especially in close quarters. Every person in the home should be trained on using it safely.

The main point in gun safety is to *always* treat a gun as if it were loaded. Never ever point a gun at something or someone you do not wish to shoot. Accidents happen all the time, so keep that muzzle pointed down and away. Since a handgun is so easy to shoot, households with children should definitely keep it under lock and key in a place inaccessible to them.

Locking away your weapon will also prevent an intruder from getting to it before *you* do. You may decide locking it up and hiding it away will keep you from reaching it in time when someone breaks in. Lots of folks say they keep a handgun right on their nightstand, next to their bed. For safety's sake, you should at least have it out unloaded, and stash your loaded clip nearby – maybe tuck it behind your nightstand or in your sock drawer. Get creative!

Remember that purchasing any gun is an investment. Common reliable handguns range from about $250 to $500, and definitely sell higher as well. Do your homework before you buy. Read articles on different handguns. Visit retail locations to inspect certain types that call to you. Ask the person at the counter to take one or several out for you, and if they can tell you more about it.

It is important to handle several guns before deciding on one, it is paramount that it feel comfortable in *your* hands. Some handguns will be too big, too small, too heavy or too light for you to fire them effectively. Everyone has their opinion on which handgun is superior, but it's just the one that works best for them. What will work best for *you*?

Talk to fellow gun owners and ask about their selection. If they happen to be a friend of yours, they might take you out to the shooting range and you could even try their guns out before committing to a purchase. You will have to consider different trigger pulls, single or double action handguns and magazine capacities, but get a *feel* for them and carry the handgun that fits you.

Shotguns – A homeowner wielding a shotgun would make any invader think twice. We see the awesome power of this weapon in movies, tearing people apart at close range. It's not a bad idea to keep one around, but it definitely has its drawbacks. It takes a little more muscle and training to handle a weapon that offers this much power.

Perhaps you have seen videos online of people firing a shotgun for the first time – the kickback can knock you right over! Another consideration is how often the shotgun can potentially jam. This tends to happen a bit more with the automatic version, so as long as you can manage a pump action successfully you should probably stick with one of those, at least initially.

You're going to have to clear that jam during combat, and make your shots count. Also, a shotgun isn't only going to destroy your enemy, it's probably going to destroy your house as well. Projectiles could pass all the way through your target, so make sure of what's behind them or next to them before unloading.

Shotguns are also great at attracting unwanted attention, as they are extremely loud. Unless your position has been thoroughly compromised and you need serious crowd control, select another firearm.

<u>Rifles</u> – A rifle is suited for long range attacks, securing your perimeter and even hunting for food. A lookout with a scoped rifle can eliminate threats at a distance or at least buy you extra time to address the situation and bugout if necessary.

AR-15s have become insanely popular with preppers, as they are fairly easy to handle and you can expend lots of rounds quickly. They're not necessarily cheap though – you're going to have to save up for this one. Combat with a rifle at closer range can be dangerous, as the bullets could pass through people and walls.

Always maintain control when firing and resist the temptation to "spray and pray". In the hands of a disciplined shooter, this weapon is surely a problem solver.

<u>Other Weapons</u>
Yes, you should definitely invest in a firearm, at least one handgun to carry with you to get you out of a potentially deadly situation. But during your survival there are many alternatives that may serve you better. Save the guns as a last resort. They require special care and handling, and no matter what they make far more noise than you would ever want to. What other weapons can you add to your arsenal?

<u>Combat Knife</u> – Your main blade should be able to defend you in combat. In addition to other blade requirements, it should be long

enough to reach the enemy and deal penetrating damage. However, its length should not make it cumbersome or difficult to wield in close quarters. In cramped spaces, you may be able to attack with your knife before the enemy can draw his gun on you and fire. Carry your knife in an easily accessible place on your body and practice drawing it from the sheath quickly and safely. Practicing will lead to muscle memory, which can bring an advantage when your adrenaline takes over.

Machete – Is bigger better? Sometimes, yes! Carrying a machete can improve your range in a fight, and the sight of one may make a would-be attacker think twice. As with any blade, your machete can also be a valuable tool and you should aim to purchase one of high quality and strength.

Crossbow – The draw of this weapon is range and stealth. Firing a bolt from a crossbow gives you a ranged attack like a firearm would. And unlike a firearm you can shoot in silence instead of drawing attention to your location. Being able to retrieve and reuse your ammunition is a significant perk of this weapon. Skilled archers can enjoy all of these benefits with a regular bow as well, the crossbow just makes it a little easier with its simple point and shoot action.

Crowbar – Ah yes, the satisfaction and reliability of blunt force. You could also reach for a medieval mace or a baseball bat if you like, but the crowbar is just straight up useful. The crowbar's appeal lies in its ability to function as a tool, which is what it is actually made for. Every group who is bugging out should probably have one for gaining entry to barricaded areas or stored items. As a weapon you can swing and bash the bad guy in, thrust at the enemy like a spear or hook them with the curved edge. All of these options have definitely made the crowbar a favorite among zombie preppers, who focus on targeting the head.

Non-Lethal Irritants – Pepper spray or mace can give you an advantage in combat or make it possible to flee. If you are unable to legally obtain pepper spray you can brew up our own at home, just ask the internet! Gel based irritants work exceptionally well because they cling to the attacker, instead of the wind blowing it back into your own eyes.

In a true survival situation, you may not be as concerned about using substances that don't do permanent damage. In that case, any sprayed chemical will do the job for you by creating distance and temporarily *or* permanently blinding your attacker. For example, investigate the wide assortment of insect repellants available on the market. Some aerosol sprays designed to kill bugs inside the home have a very focused stream, and sprays meant for taking out wasp nests will definitely give you the range you need to stay safe.

In the old days, ninjas used finely ground glass blown into an enemy's eyes to destroy his sight. Anything in the eyes is going to slow your opponent down, for sure. But if you do decide you want something that only incapacitates and does not *harm* an enemy, go grab a high capacity squirt gun and try out some do-it-yourself concoctions. At the very least it should be a memorable afternoon.

Incendiaries – For the record, you should avoid fighting with fire whenever possible. Flames are not something you can easily control, and can quickly spread to structures or property you do not wish to burn. Flamethrowers, Molotov cocktails and other fiery weapons will definitely draw attention and make a mess of things. Whether to use flames in combat should be left up to the most level-headed, conservative person in your group. If you do want to explore the creation of incendiaries, a prepper might want to keep some lighter fluid or alcohol-based sanitizer around. Hand sanitizer is especially cheap, flammable and easy to carry. You may be able to squirt it out of the bottle onto the enemy or coat projectiles with it. At the very least, it should help when you're having trouble getting a campfire going.

Tools and Other Gear

You never know what you may encounter in a survival situation. Maybe you're bugging in and decide to board up the windows. Maybe you bugged out on your mountain bike and it's in need of repair. Or you've been living in the forest for the past month and you want to fashion a spear for hunting.

Between your home, your bugout bag and your survival caches you may want to add tools and other gear to help you through tough situations and solve problems. Consider what you might want to add to your supplies as space and weight restrictions allow. The following items are mainly supplemental to your other preps. Anything considered to be mandatory will also be found in the other supply lists.

- Multi-tool – They come in all shapes and sizes, and you can acquire one or several to cover your bases.

- Flashlight – You will absolutely need light when the power goes out. In addition to the traditional flashlight you can also use a lantern or strap on a head lamp to keep your hands free.

- Paracord – A strong length of parachute cord, often sold as woven bracelets that you can unravel when you need it. It will hold up as well as any rope and won't take up space in your bugout bag.

- Collapsible or multi-function shovel – Digging trenches will definitely be easier if you have an actual shovel. Camping shovels are collapsible and lightweight, allowing them to travel with you. Some shovels have sharp edges or serrations to perform other tasks, and some even have bottle openers!

- Duct tape – Duct tape can solve any problem. Whether you're patching the roof of your tent or building a raft, you're going to need duct tape.

- Multiple fire starters – Fire is key to staying fed and keeping warm. You should *always* have several ways of making fire in case you lose your lighter. Carry extra lighters as well as waterproof matches and a magnesium striker. Have fire starters with every jacket and bag, as well as in your car. Keep small batches of tinder as well – dryer lint smeared with petroleum jelly or a few pieces of char cloth stored in a medicine bottle or small tin will get your fire blazing fast.

- Compass and map of surrounding area – If you bug out into the thick of the wilderness or into the next town, it can't hurt to have a guide of the area. Having a secondary location to bug out to is your ultimate goal, and you need to make sure everyone can get there even if they *think* they know the way.

- Small bags – Plastic sandwich baggies are great for keeping small items together and dry. There are also polyester bags available that will guarantee protection from water damage and make less noise. The polyester bags will also be reusable indefinitely.

- Sewing kit – A missing button is not that big of a deal, but in a prolonged survival situation your clothes may eventually be reduced to rags. Even without actual sewing *skills*, you can manage to patch up a few holes or stick a button on with some needle and thread. If you have the time, however, learn how to sew. It's definitely a prepper skill!

- Sleeping pad – When you bug out you can certainly sleep on the ground if you have to. You may opt for a sleeping bag or a bed roll that's as light as possible. A sleeping pad can keep you off the cold, wet ground and boost your comfort level. And when bugging in you may acquire a few guests, so consider having a sleeping pad or air mattress and some extra bedding in the home.

- Fasteners and binders – You don't want to burn through all your duct tape, right? Include some other little items like safety pins, elastic bands, key chain rings and zip ties. They won't add any weight or bulk to your bugout bag, and you can even carry them in your pockets if you like.

- Wearable items – Like paracord bracelets or the addition of some extra safety pins to your jacket, any tool you can wear will provide more room in the bugout bag – and make it far easier to access than rifling through your bag all the time. You can find small tools and flashlights that can be worn around the neck, and compasses get attached to just about everything imaginable. You can fashion your own necklace for an item or even hang small tools off of your belt. Just remember to keep it all functional, quiet and out of the way of your weapons.

- Two way radios – If you're traveling with a group or make a friend out there, you might want to or *have* to communicate at a distance. If you split up to find food or are patrolling your perimeter, having a radio can keep you efficient and keep you safe. Remember to keep your volume low, and silence your radio if you're being hunted.

- Plywood and nails – If you have a space to store some plywood, two by fours, hammer and nails, you'll definitely have an easier time in the long run. You can board up windows, build barricades, repair your structure or fashion a new one. If you have a garage or secondary location, it can be a smart investment for the apocalypse.

- Fire extinguisher – The last thing you need is for your house to burn to the ground when society has already collapsed around you. A perfectly good shelter with everything you need deserves to be maintained and protected. Always follow fire safety precautions, doomsday or not. You've worked hard for your supplies, take care of what's yours by keeping a fire extinguisher at your primary and secondary locations.

- Can openers – Just like fire starters, you should keep more than one can opener around in case one gets lost or it breaks. It doesn't take long for a manual cranking can opener to break or jam up. You should keep a couple of those in the home, but also use the military style can openers that can punch through metal. They are one piece of metal with no mechanisms to break, small and easy to tuck in a pocket or bag. And as far as cans go, buy the self-opening ones with the pull tab whenever possible.

- Generator – In many disasters it is possible your home will lose power. In the apocalypse, the power's not coming back anytime soon. Having a generator will keep your lights on and the refrigerator running. There are generators that run on multiple fuels or solar powered models, which can be a great backup.

- Rechargeable batteries and solar powered charger – When there's no electricity you're going to turn to your battery operated devices, especially flashlights. Rechargeable batteries have come a long way and last much longer than they used to. Having a solar charging station will keep them going, and you can also get solar chargers for cell phones and other small electrical items. If the sun's still coming up every morning, you might as well use it.

- Fuel and fuel pump – Cars and gasoline generators will require fuel or they will become useless junk. Stockpiling gasoline is doable, but requires appropriate storage space and rotation, as gas can deteriorate in as little as three months. There are additives to help the shelf life of your gasoline, but you should also have a siphon on hand when you need to scavenge for gas on the road.

- Activated charcoal – This stuff can be found in capsule form in the vitamin section of many stores. People ingest the capsules to purify their insides, but activated charcoal can purify just about anything – including the water you drink and the air you breathe. Filtering water through charcoal can help to decontaminate a found water source you need to drink from. You can even fashion your very own "gas masks" by layering face masks used for house painting with ground up charcoal, making it easier to breathe through airborne chemicals and particles.

- Hacksaw and bolt cutters – In addition to tightening screws or loosening nuts, you may have to cut through some stuff. There are some things you're not going to be able to cut through with your survival knife. Having a saw and cutters can help you build shelter or gain access through fences and chains.

- Heirloom seeds and gardening tools – If things get out of hand for too long, and you have to wait for society to rebuild itself, growing a garden can sustain you in the meantime. Having your own food means fewer supply runs that become less fruitful and more dangerous as time goes on. Keeping heirloom seeds will produce fruits and vegetables that develop new seeds for future planting. Study up on how to grow your own food and which plants are best suited for your climate.

- Candles – Everyone should have candles in case the power goes out, even if they think preppers are insane and there's nothing to prepare for. Tea light candles don't burn long but they are small, easy to carry and you can buy them in bulk. There are also long-burning candles which are usually coiled beeswax, which can last up to 60 hours. Just make sure you do have candles and use them safely, away from flammable items.

Clothes to Survive In

During times of survival, fashion takes a back seat to comfort and utility. Nobody is going to care if your clothes are wrinkled and your outfit doesn't match. Maintaining your personal comfort for as long as possible will keep you going through the tough stuff. Being appropriately dressed for your environment and keeping your body protected are vital and should be given consideration. It's definitely easier to select your wardrobe before a disaster, so keep these points in mind during your preps.

Footwear should be appropriate for long hikes and should already be broken in. You must be able to move at a moment's notice, and nothing will slow you down like blisters on your achy, tired feet.

Wearing layers will allow you to adapt to changing temperatures, and is especially recommended in cold weather over wearing one thicker layer. An example of an outfit for warm and cool temps might include a long sleeved shirt, undershirt, hooded weatherproof jacket with removable liner and pants that can also zip off to shorts.

Your hairstyle may undergo some changes if you find yourself in a prolonged battle for survival. What people find attractive is often not the most practical. Shorter hair definitely requires less brushing and detangling, not to mention harder for someone to grab you by and better for hotter climates. But before you go shaving your head realize that your scalp can definitely suffer from sunburn and may require sunscreen or a hat. In a colder climate longer hair can retain body heat even better than just a hat, although both would be ideal.

Utility and protection are your main concerns. Sunglasses and a handkerchief will aid you whether it is hot or cold outside. Sporting a belt could save a life later if someone needs a tourniquet. Work gloves can save your hands when you're climbing a jagged mountainside or collecting firewood. A jacket or vest for tactical purposes or outdoor recreation will provide you with plenty of pockets to carry all your little survival tools and free up space in your backpack.

Keeping a Low Profile

Whether you're bugging in at home or making camp out in the wilderness, keeping a low profile is your best defense. There may be looters, gangs or even the undead out on the prowl, and you may not be equipped to take them all on. You should always sweep your perimeter for potential threats, but try to do so without drawing attention. The best way to get noticed is to be seen and heard, so unless you're flagging down a rescue helicopter, try to remain undetected.

Be Invisible – Make sure you see them before they see you. Try to wear drab, muted colors and if possible match them to the colors of your surroundings. Camouflage comes in many different color patterns to lower visibility in different terrains. Traditional green forest camo isn't going to help you in the snow or the desert. Some people even construct ghillie suits, which are outfits matching the color of your terrain and have the surrounding natural vegetation added to them.

The purpose of these suits is to blend into the environment and break up the recognizable outline of the human body. Whatever you decide to wear, avoid bright, contrasting colors if you want to avoid detection. Sadly, if you've just dyed your hair bright neon blue, you're going to stand out in all the wrong ways. You'll have to cover your hair up when you're out in the open. Maybe you could just shave your head and start over!

Take off anything sparkly or flashy that could reflect the sun's rays, such as a wristwatch or a shiny gold necklace. At home, cover your windows – with blackout curtains if possible. At night, use low light or no light if you can get by without it. When there's no power and you *do* need light, keep it dim with a small tea light candle or even a glow stick if that's all you need. If you have a basement or other room without windows, you can use it for your nighttime tasks where light is necessary.

Disable any motion detectors or timers on your lights at home – you are not trying to scare off a petty burglar anymore, you are trying to conceal yourself from extremely dangerous and violent criminals in what might be an abandoned neighborhood! When bugging out, make a fire when you must for cooking or warmth, but keep it small and have someone posted as lookout until you can extinguish it.

If you just need a fire for cooking, relocate and sleep in a different area when you are done. Maybe you can do without a fire for warmth by using reflective emergency blankets that will trap the heat from your body. If you are with other people, consider them a resource and by all means snuggle up together for warmth. You might not even like each other, but be prepared to get a *little* uncomfortable if you want to survive!

<u>Be Quiet</u> – Reduce noise by speaking softly and whisper when you suspect danger. Avoid wearing chains or jewelry and remove loose change or keys from your pockets. You can even remove zipper pulls from jackets and backpacks to reduce noise while moving.

Silence your handgun or opt for a combat knife or machete to defend yourself while patrolling. Mute cell phones, radios, home phones and even alarm clocks that may go off at inopportune moments. Does your wristwatch have an alarm? You'd better disable it. Control your reactions and resist crying out in surprise.

Maybe a mouse skittered over your foot, or you tripped over a log and fell. Scan the path you are walking as well as looking ahead to avoid being startled. If the baby is crying and you know danger is close, your best option may be to flick a few drops of water in their face – it doesn't hurt them and has been known to snap them right out of it. Finally, have medicines on hand to stop coughs and sneezes when stealth is required. You have to be quiet when it counts.

A Survival Mentality

Your outlook on a situation alone can determine whether you survive. There are countless stories of people who endured the impossible with no sign of rescue, but they never gave up hope. You have to believe that your situation may change, keeping your mind active and positive.

In a worst case scenario you may find yourself starving, freezing, or dealing with a crippling injury, but your attitude towards your predicament will determine how your story ends. Fight for your life, always look for opportunities to improve your situation- *believe* that you will make it through.

You will have to rely on your wits and endurance if you go it alone, but what if you have someone there by your side? Your chances of surviving can improve with other people, but they must also have the right mindset. When times get tough, you will have to lift each other up. Enduring a harsh existence for any prolonged amount of time can make a person just want to give up.

Let's face facts. Someone in your group may have an emotional breakdown from exhaustion, starvation, dehydration, isolation, boredom, anxiety, missing friends or relatives or even witnessing a death. Physical discomfort from small things such as sweating, chafing, itching, muscle fatigue, headaches and not bathing can take a considerable toll after awhile, and not everyone is as strong as you are.

They're thinking about hot showers, home cooked meals and video games. They don't want to walk another mile, they don't want to spend another night going hungry. You can't change the circumstances you are in. What else can you do to improve their situation?

- Distract from discomfort by stopping to do a gear check or gathering resources like firewood.
- Play a mental game like I Spy or Twenty Questions.
- Give them a sip of water.
- Have something to read to take their focus off the situation.
- Sing to them and have them join in.
- Bring physical comfort by holding them, giving hugs or scratching their back. When you make camp you might even trade foot massages. Whatever feels good!
- Let them cry or break down for a moment to release their frustrations.
- Compromise – agree to rest for a few minutes before climbing that next hill. Let them take first watch so they can have uninterrupted sleep for the night.
- Point out all the positives in whatever you're doing, and make them feel like they've really gotten something when you bargain with them.

- Taking some action, even if it doesn't solve the problem, may still have a positive effect in that there is a sense of accomplishment and control.
- Letting them come up with a solution on their own might boost their confidence as well, when they are feeling so helpless.
- A person suffering from withdrawals of any substance is going through a lot, give them lots of praise for how well they are doing and occupy their mind when cravings take hold.
- Just simply talk to them and remind them of what is necessary from all of you to survive.

Certain disasters may not be over quickly. A complete economic collapse, an EMP event, or a worldwide zombie infestation will change your day to day life considerably. You've been prepping, taking care of you and yours- how else can you make yourself useful?

If you wind up living in an apocalypse, having what others need can definitely improve your situation. Having certain items to barter and trade with could prolong your existence considerably. Eventually everyone will have to resort to scavenging for supplies in homes, warehouses, and abandoned stores. As these areas are cleared out, people will become desperate for supplies.

With your stockpiles you can help others, obtain items you need – and possibly even make a deal for your life if you fall prey to marauders. These bartering items are a little different from your other preps. They are mainly comfort items, addictive substances that people crave, and some are essentials for people in certain situations.

If you can discipline yourself to exist without these crutches and niceties, you stand to profit when the world ends. (Learning to live with less is an essential prepper skill.) Even if you are on a limited budget, you can still accumulate a few of these items- you may want to just specialize in one or two. You can also hold off on purchasing these items and simply be on the lookout when you wake up in the apocalypse, seeing these treasures for what they really are.

- Coffee, caffeine pills, energy drinks and shots
- Cigarettes and alcohol
- Chocolate – other sweets as well, especially since chocolate can melt or go stale, but that's why it will be a rare treat and a huge morale booster
- Quality soaps and moisturizers, fresh razors, shampoo (save those bottles from the hotel), lip balm, sunscreen
- Extra clothing such as cotton tees and socks
- Baby items like diapers, baby wipes and formula
- Quality toilet paper, feminine napkins and tampons
- Medicine for colds and seasonal allergies, pain relievers, bandages and multivitamins
- Gasoline, propane and motor oil
- Lighters, flashlights and batteries

Hidden Caches

In case of a bugout situation it may be wise to have hidden caches of supplies near your home, on the way to your target destination, and at your target destination. Items can be stored in a weatherproof container for future access, usually buried in the ground or concealed in a secret spot that is well camouflaged.

These stores should only be emergency supplies to replace what may have been consumed or left behind. If you were forced to abandon your home or your supplies were stolen or destroyed, a cache can keep you going for a few days. Your biggest collection of backup supplies should be in the vicinity of your bugout location, where you plan to regroup, make camp and fortify your base.

There are many containers available to consider for your cache, the most economical would be a plastic container with a snap on lid. Contents inside your container which are perishable or vulnerable to the elements should be placed in sealed plastic bags. To further protect your supplies you should seal your container with duct tape before burying or concealing it. Consider how easy it will be to retrieve your items.

If you bury the cache, you must be able to get at it, even if you lose your shovel or the ground is frozen. You should do your best to cover the spot with materials natural to the area, such as branches, tall grasses or rocks. Make sure it looks natural, no obvious signs of a manmade, precise layout of material. However you hide it, you must make sure that no one else will possibly discover it.

You will lose your supplies and could potentially give away your location to looters. While you must hide your container well, you must also ensure that you WILL be able to find it again! What could be worse than being in a desperate situation on the run and having what you need but not being able to retrieve it? Pick a location you are familiar with or become very well acquainted with this location.

Maybe you have a secluded spot in the woods which is off the path, or you know of an abandoned field which is not appropriate for development. Your spot should be well known to you, but not to others. Find something off trail, in the rough, concealed with natural vegetation.

Your emergency cache should ideally be within a day's hike from your home. Walk to this location from your home, take different routes and really KNOW the way to your supplies. A map can certainly help and you may share your cache location with the trusted people you plan to bugout with.

Obviously if there are changes to your group you may wish to relocate your cache if you fear they may steal or sabotage your supplies- only tell who you must. The primary items listed would be appropriate for your emergency bugout cache which you would visit after leaving your home or desperately needed a resupply while bugging in. The secondary items are a great reserve to include in additional caches further out, on your way to your backup location.

PRIMARY CACHE ITEMS

- Toilet paper, wrapped in plastic – small items can be stored in the tubes
- Bottled water and canteen
- Water purification tablets or filter
- Nonperishable food, also a can opener if including canned items
- Duplicate of your primary medical kit
- Lighter, waterproof matches and char cloth/dryer lint
- Paracord
- Multi-tool
- Compass and map of surrounding area
- Survival knife for camping/outdoors which can double as a combat knife
- Ammunition for bugout firearm(s)
- Flashlight
- Duct tape
- Pair of socks

SECONDARY CACHE ITEMS

- Heirloom seeds which when planted will produce new seeds

- Flares and signaling mirror
- Batteries for any flashlights or other devices you may use or find in the future
- More toilet paper, food and water, you can never have enough
- Small toolkit including screwdrivers, pliers, and a wire saw
- Solar powered or hand crank radio
- Survival/pocket knife
- Backup weapon such as a combat knife, machete, crowbar
- Tarp or plastic sheeting for rudimentary protection from the elements
- Container for gathering and boiling water
- Compact shovel
- Secondary medical kit

<u>Drills and Dry Runs</u>

You may find it beneficial to implement some survival drills, so that when the time comes you know exactly what you need to do and how to get it done efficiently. Even the simplest thing like knowing where your family will meet up in the event of a house fire can be a disaster if you don't discuss it beforehand and try it out.

Everyone involved must be in agreement, move quickly and decisively, and know the possible pitfalls and obstacles. What harm is there in conducting a drill? Absolutely none, do NOT feel silly for trying to ensure your continued survival! If you and your loved ones know exactly what to do when a tornado siren goes off or there is a citywide blackout, you already have a distinct advantage in a disaster, even if you do not stock extra supplies.

Your neighbors will say they don't have time for a plan and a drill, or that the disaster will never happen. You should do your best to make sure your people aren't the ones running around lost in a panic, terrified and vulnerable- make a plan! Not to mention that out of all the prepping you may do, practicing safety drills is the cheapest. You don't need equipment, hoarded supplies or funding, it is free. So, what sort of questions do we need to answer when considering a survival drill?

- Which events should you bug in for and which should you bug out for? For instance, you will probably be bugging in during a tornado and bugging out during a fire.

- What supplies do you need to grab and where will they be located? You may want to grab a flashlight and a radio if heading to your basement. If you need to leave, bugout bags should be prepped and in place.

- Where can the members of your household/group meet up if your home is compromised and you need to bug out? Maybe head for the street light at the corner, your neighbor's yard, or the gas station a few blocks away. You MUST be in agreement on this, and it should be idiot-proof- not "100 yards past the big oak tree and then 50 paces west". Pick a landmark you all know that even a child left on their own could find.

- What can you do to protect your home during the disaster? In the event of looting and riots you should lock doors, cover windows and prepare to barricade entry points. If your house is threatened by wildfires, you should close your windows and start watering your roof. Visualize the disaster and what it will *threaten*.

- What can you do to protect yourselves during the disaster? Do your children know how to call 911 and what they should say? Is there a firearm in the house and is everyone trained on proper handling and use?

- What sort of dry runs would help you prepare? How long would it take you to pack everyone in the van and drive to the nearest grocery store? What will it be like when you have to help each other into the hazmat suits? Just what exactly is it going to take to get your survival raft inflated and in the water?

Every step you take towards preparedness will make you a strong and skilled survivor. Remember why you are doing these drills. You can "look stupid" doing dry runs and making your family run around for nothing, or you can *definitely* look stupid when you stand helpless in horror as it finally hits the fan. Don't be that guy.

Well, there you have it.

Hopefully reviewing these tips will make you a more confident and successful prepper. In the end your own ingenuity and growing knowledge will keep you alive in any situation and will cost you very little. Focus on learning skills and practicing techniques with what you have, while aiming to save for tomorrow.

Read about prepping and all kinds of stories of survival. Get out there and meet some fellow preppers as well. Most of them are happy to give advice and share a few of their secrets. Without a sense of community, we will be truly lost in the wake of devastation. Some of us will have to work to rebuild society and lend a helping hand to those in need, which makes prepping a most noble hobby indeed.

Hopefully nothing bad will ever happen to you, but if things do take a turn for the worse, you *can* survive!

Good luck, fellow preppers!

*****

If you've enjoyed this book, **please** consider leaving a review and letting others know what you thought!

www.ingramcontent.com/pod-product-compliance
Lightning Source LLC
Chambersburg PA
CBHW070916290526
45795CB00001B/328